TECHNOLOGY IN ACTION

MEDICAL TECHNOLOGY

Jenny Bryan

Wayland

Titles in this series

Aircraft Technology

Building Technology

Camera Technology

Car Technology

Energy Technology

Farming Technology

Food Technology

Information Technology

Medical Technology

Military Technology

Ship Technology

Spacecraft Technology

Sport Technology

Train Technology

TV and Video Technology

Undersea Technology

First published in 1991 by
Wayland (Publishers) Ltd
61 Western Road, Hove
East Sussex BN3 1JD, England

Editor: Paul Mason
Designer: Alison Anholt-White / David Armitage

British Library Cataloguing in Publication Data
Bryan, Jenny
Medical technology
1. Medicine. Technological innovation
I. Title. II. Series
610

ISBN 1-85210-936-X

Typeset by Direct Image Photosetting Limited, Sussex, England
Printed in Italy by G. Canale & C.S.p.A., Turin
Bound in France by A.G.M.

Cover Surgeons performing microsurgery using powerful microscopes to see what they are doing.

Contents

1 A century of technology

This century has been one of discovery in medicine. Advances in technology have played an important part in all the most exciting developments: antibiotics, open heart surgery, dialysis, transplants, body scanners, lasers.

Some of the foundations for these advances were laid even before the dawn of the new century. The first use of X-rays by Wilhelm Roentgen was in 1895. Earlier still came Louis Pasteur's crucial work on micro-organisms. These and other nineteenth century developments helped put medicine on a much more scientific footing than before. Doctors were starting to question theories – many of them quite wrong – that had governed the way they had been treating their patients.

As this century has progressed, so has the pace of technological advance. Computers have slashed the time spent doing the everyday drudgery of scientific research – the endless calculations, checked and re-checked. Instead, scientists can spend more of their time on the really innovative work that brings the breakthroughs.

Ideas that were pure fantasy only ten or fifteen years ago are fast becoming reality: babies conceived in the laboratory; organs and tissues, hopelessly damaged by accident or disease, repaired or replaced.

Technology has helped to improve the quality as well as the length of life for people with long-term conditions such as diabetes, asthma, and arthritis. To the cancer patient, the automatic pump which drips vital drugs into the bloodstream and relieves pain is just as much a breakthrough as the multi-million pound machine which diagnosed a tumour in the first place.

But many challenges remain. Can we halt the physical and mental deterioration which comes with old age? And what hope is there for those people paralysed by accident or disease whose severed nerves are beyond the scope of current surgery? What hope for children born with disabilities, or adolescents unable to lead the life they would like because of inherited disorders? These are some of the people who are still waiting for the technology which can help them. They are still waiting for tomorrow's discoveries.

Louis Pasteur's work on fermentation established him as one of the founders of modern medicine. He is shown in his laboratory.

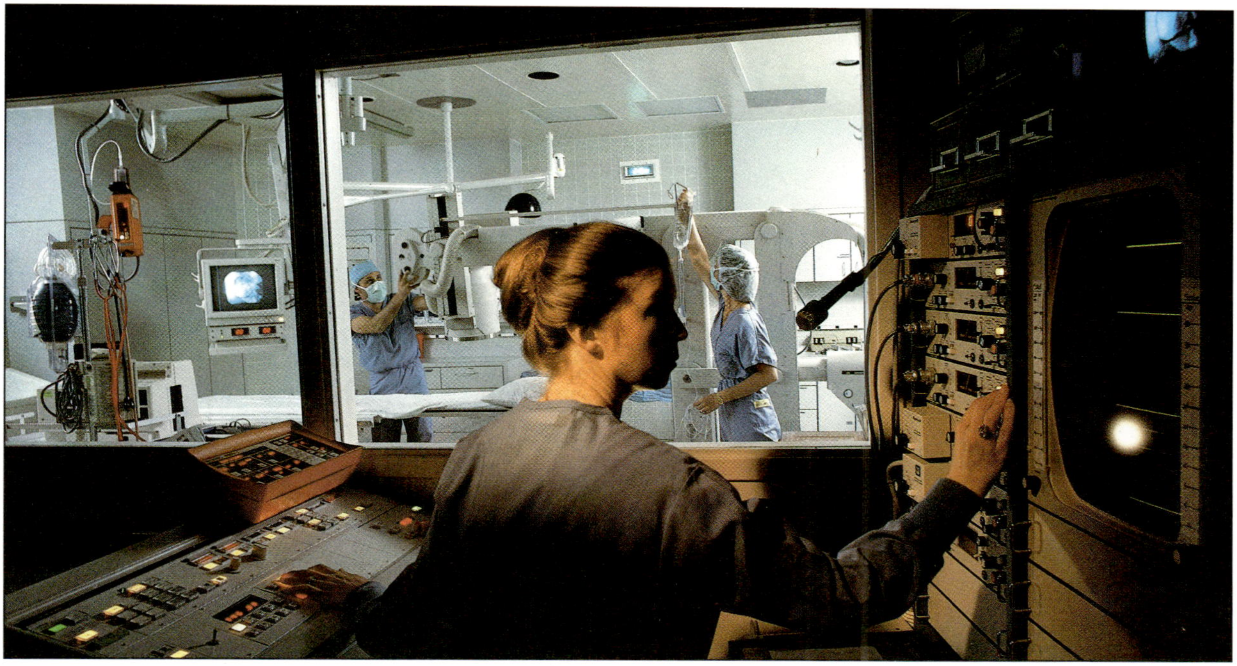

Above Today's operating theatres are full of technology and are kept scrupulously clean to make sure that patients are not exposed to sources of infection which could slow down their recovery.

Compare the scene above with this nineteenth century operating theatre, which really looks like a theatre! The only concession to hygiene appears to be that the doctors are wearing white jackets.

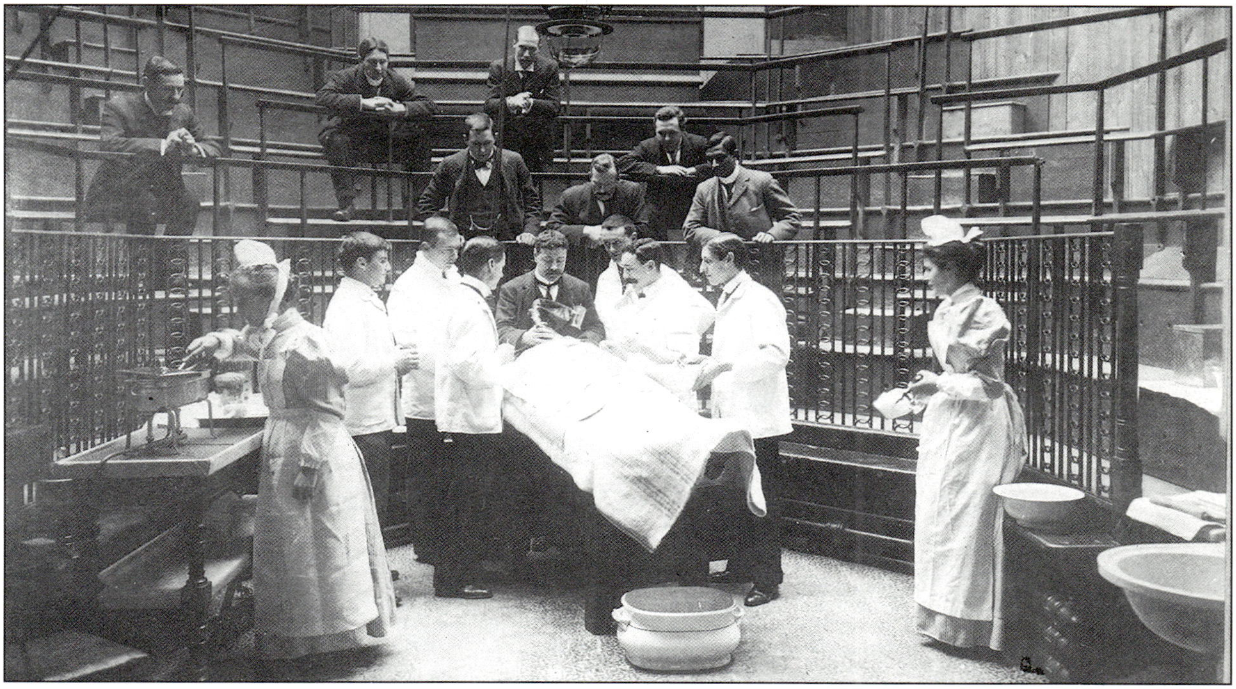

2 Windows into the body

Wilhelm Roentgen's first X-ray – a fuzzy picture of his wife's hand – was just the start of a revolution in ways to diagnose illness. This revolution means that, today, surgeons rarely have to reach for their scalpels to find out what is wrong with someone.

Those so called 'exploratory operations' have largely been replaced by investigations which use computer-controlled X-rays, sound waves and even huge magnetic fields to take detailed pictures of what is happening deep inside the body.

Right X-rays make a picture on a photographic plate because they are absorbed by different tissues in different amounts, so more of them end up on one part of the plate than another.

Left Early X-ray machines were very different from today's sophisticated devices. Here, Wilhelm Roentgen holds a photographic plate behind a young patient to get an image of his lungs.

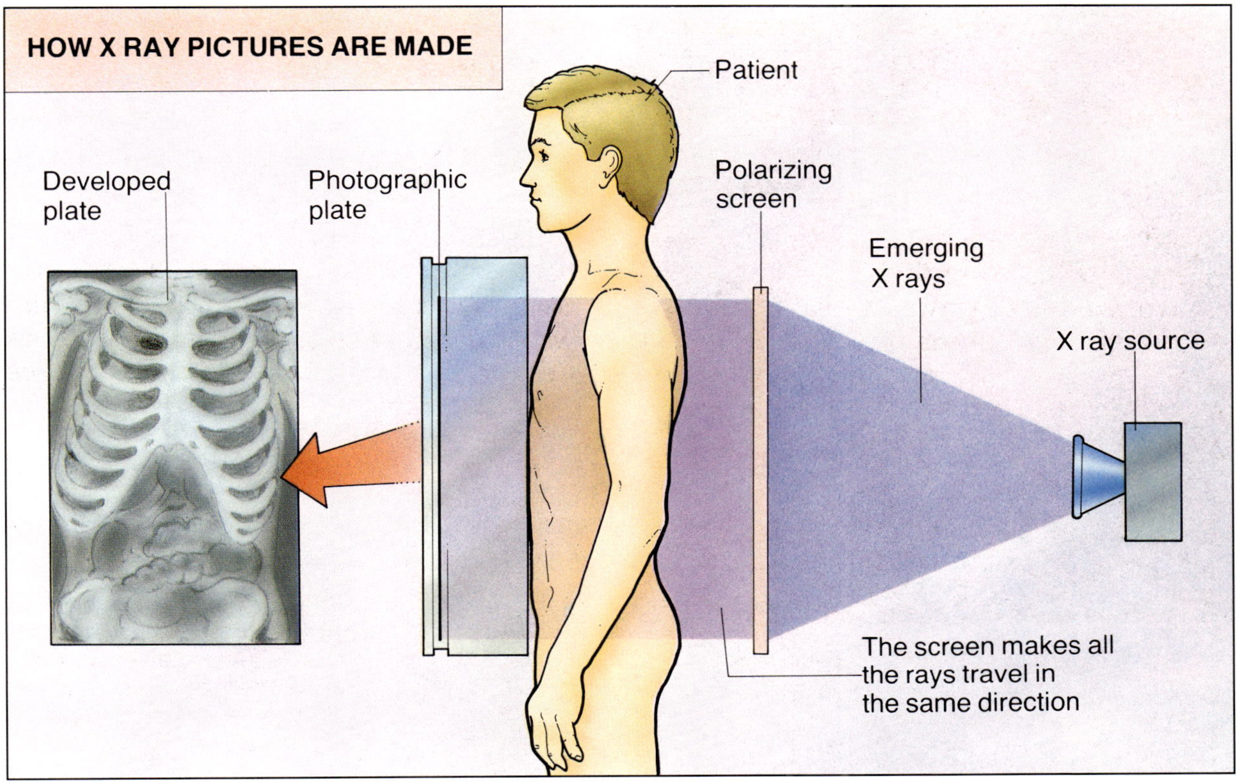

Simple X-rays are still used for many routine investigations to find out, for example, if a bone is broken or a lung infected. The familiar white-on-black image is produced when X-rays are passed through the body. The amount of the rays absorbed by the different tissues depends on their density. Unabsorbed rays pass straight through the body and blacken the photographic plate placed behind the patient. Bones, which are made of the most dense material, appear white because they absorb a lot of rays. So very few are left to blacken the photographic plate. In contrast, fat is very watery and does not absorb many X-rays. The result is a black image which is hard to distinguish from other soft tissues.

In some cases a better picture can be obtained by injecting a dye into the blood passing through the tissue that is being examined. This makes the blood vessels show up better and is called angiography.

In computerized tomography (CT) scanning, developed during the early 1970s, dozens of X-rays are passed through the body at different angles. Computers can then measure the amount of X-rays absorbed by each tissue. This data is converted into accurate pictures of thin 'slices' of tissue, often only a few millimetres thick. This enables doctors to see tumours, blood clots and other small abnormalities which would be invisible to ordinary X-ray machines.

A further refinement is to store X-ray pictures on computer both before and after dyes are injected. The computer then 'subtracts' the first picture from the second to highlight, for example, blocks in blood vessels.

Although X-rays are very useful for getting pictures of the inside of the body, they do carry certain risks. Pregnant women cannot have X-rays because it is highly likely that they would damage the fetus. Nor are X-rays much good at getting detailed pictures of tissues such as fat.

CT scans, such as this one, enable doctors to see a 'slice' of a patient's body.

During the 1940s and 1950s researchers began to use sound waves to try and get pictures of the inside of the body. Sound waves inaudible to the human ear were bounced off the internal organs. The 'echoes' which were picked up as they left the body varied in strength according to the kind of tissue they had bounced off.

The technique took years to perfect. But by the late 1960s and early 1970s ultrasound was gradually being accepted as a valuable diagnostic tool. Since then it has been used routinely to scan pregnant women in the world's rich countries, to check that the fetus is growing normally.

In the most skilled hands, ultrasound can be used to detect tiny but potentially fatal abnormalities in the fetus. The parents can then be given the chance to abort it. Or, where possible, preparations can be made for corrective surgery immediately after birth or even in the womb.

Below Ultrasound scanning of pregnant women for fetal abnormalities such as spina bifida or heart defects is done routinely in many countries, among them China.

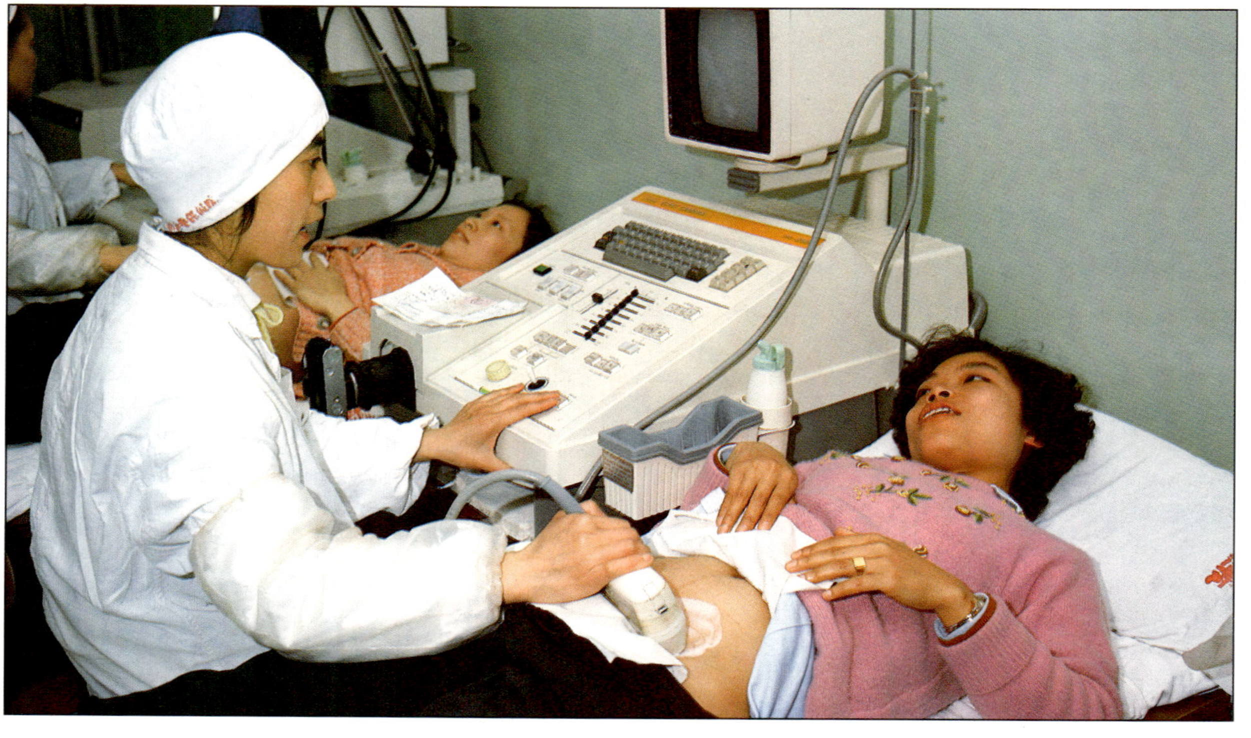

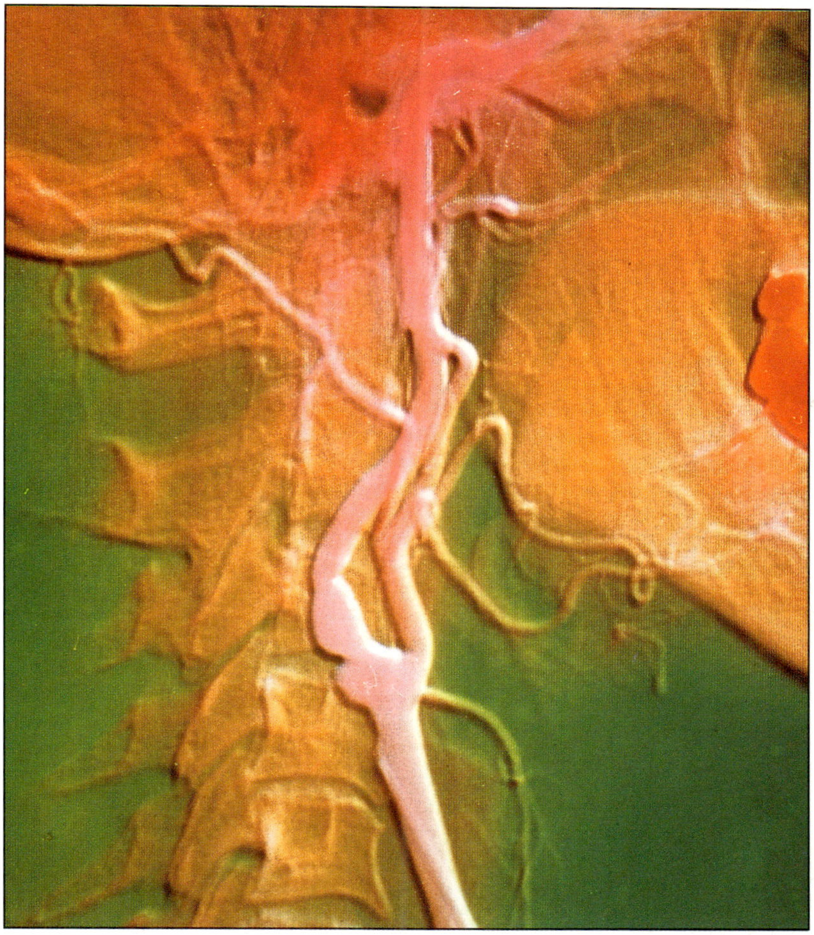

Images such as this false colour angiogram make it much easier for doctors to find out what is wrong with people.

The most recent addition to the high-tech investigations available to doctors is magnetic resonance imaging (MRI). This makes use of the fact that much of the body is made of water and therefore contains huge quantities of hydrogen atoms. Put hydrogen atoms in a large magnetic field and bombard them with harmless radio waves and they get very excited!

Switch off the radio waves and each hydrogen atom will release a small amount of energy in the form of a faint radio signal. A computer can convert these signals into a picture according to the type and strength of the signal. So a piece of fatty tissue with a lot of water will appear quite different from bone, which contains very little.

The quality of pictures produced by MRI scanning has improved dramatically since the technique was first used in the early 1980s. It can now be used to diagnose anything from heart disease to cancer, multiple sclerosis to birth defects.

None of these techniques – X-rays, CT scanning, ultrasound or MRI – can, on its own, satisfy all the diagnostic demands of doctors. Instead, these methods complement each other. Some are better for diagnosing particular illnesses than others.

Doctors also have to consider cost. CT and MRI machines are hugely expensive to buy and run. There is little point in using them when a simple X-ray would do the job just as well. Clearly, there is still a lot for doctors to learn about the best way to open the windows into the body.

3 Looking down hollow tubes

Imagine the advantages of being able to look down a telescope and see inside the human body. That is what surgeons can now do, thanks to advances in fibreoptic technology. Fortunately, patients do not have to swallow a whole telescope. Instead, a flexible tube, about the width of your finger, can be passed up or down virtually any of the hollow passageways of the body. Inside the tube are thousands of fine glass or plastic fibres that carry light down into the body and illuminate the place which the doctor wants to look at. Other groups of fibres carry an image of this spot back up to the eyepiece, through which the doctor is looking.

For example, a fibreoptic tube can be inserted into the mouth and carefully wiggled down the throat, into the stomach and down into the intestine. This tube is called an endoscope. On the way down, the doctor can check the oesophagus – the tube that carries food from the mouth to the stomach. Inflammation, ulcers, bleeding, or abnormal growths will be clearly visible.

If the doctor sees anything suspicious he or she can insert a probe on a long wire down the tube and extract a tiny sample of tissue which can be examined under a microscope for problems. Similar fibreoptic tubes can look down the airways into the lungs, as well as the lower parts of the intestine and the female reproductive tract.

A FIBREOPTIC TUBE

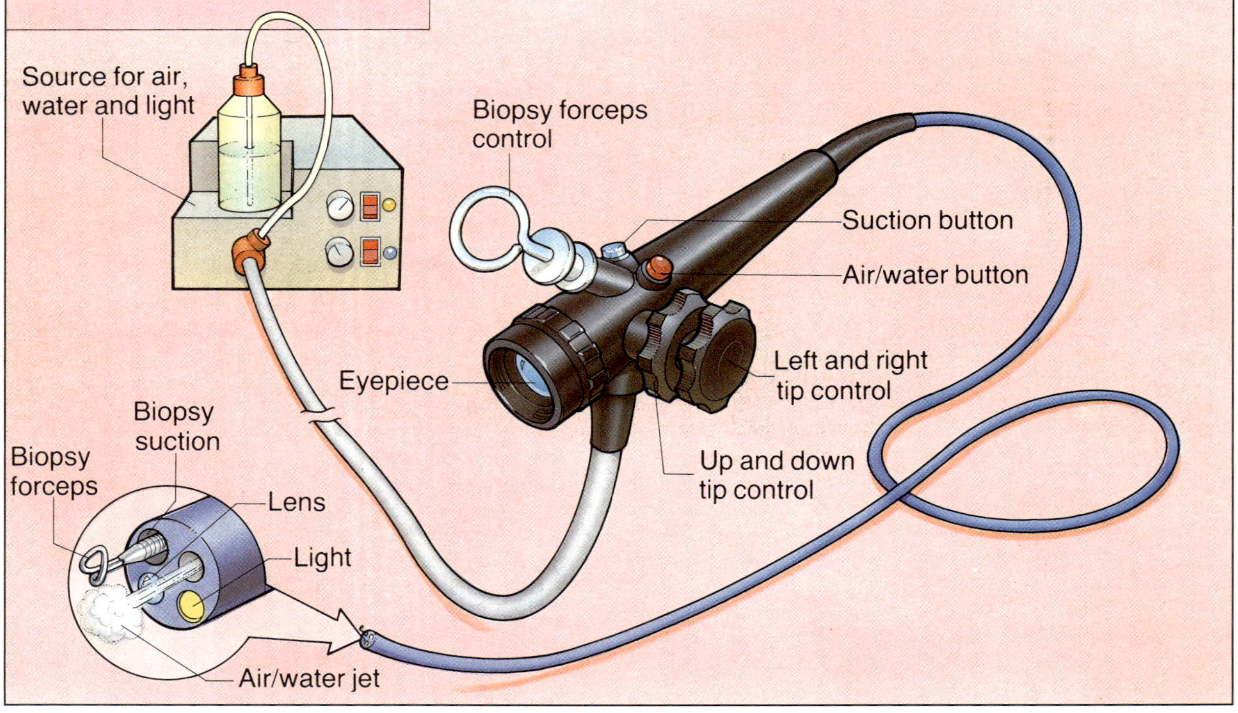

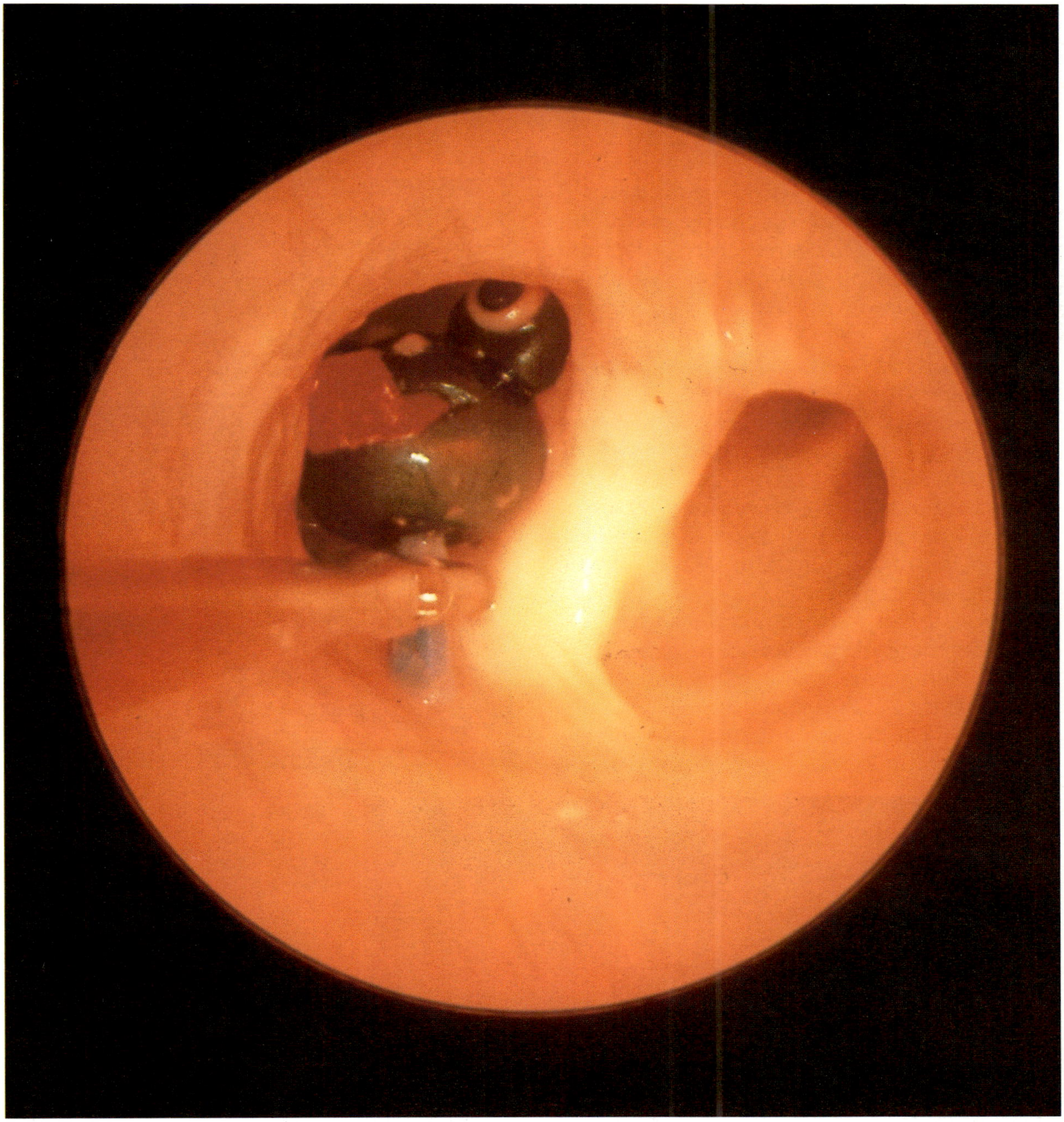

A new meaning for the phrase 'frog in your throat'! Looking down an endoscope the surgeon can see and remove the drink stirrer that is stuck there. This means that there is no need to operate.

All these examinations can be done without a general anaesthetic, though patients are often given drugs to help them relax while the fibreoptic tube is being inserted.

The view which results is remarkable. Every twist and turn of the body's internal plumbing is on show; nothing stays hidden from the doctor's penetrating gaze.

4 Keyhole surgery

Once scanners and fibreoptics made it possible to diagnose so many conditions without the need for exploratory operations, surgeons began to look at how they might decrease the amount of major surgery needed in treatment.

The result has been a big shift, over the last twenty years, away from dramatic and often drastic surgery towards smaller operations, which put right problems but cause little damage to healthy tissue nearby.

Many operations are now done under local instead of general anaesthetic. Patients recover more quickly and leave hospital earlier. Some can even go home the same day. Less time spent in hospital means a smaller risk of catching an infection and a faster return to work and normal home life.

The secret of this success has been the increasing use of 'keyhole' surgery. Entering the body through the tiniest of incisions, the

Above Until the nineteenth century patients were lucky to escape from an operation with their life!

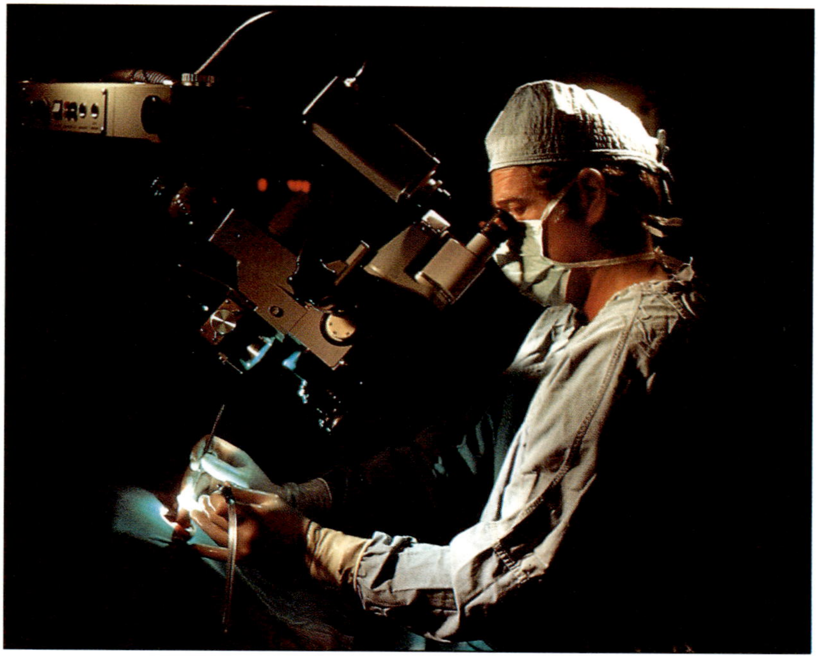

Left Today, surgeons can operate on the tiniest blood vessels and nerves, thanks to microscopes and miniature scalpels.

Thanks to keyhole surgery, many athletes whose careers would previously have been ended by injury can now continue to compete, because the operations on damaged tissue are so minor.

surgeon works with miniature operating instruments and uses high-power binoculars to see what he or she is doing.

Many operations on major organs, bones, blood vessels and even nerves are now performed in this way. A woman having fertility treatment can have eggs removed from her ovaries through a tiny cut in her abdomen. A young athlete can have damaged cartilage removed from the knee through a small hole in the joint, thus minimizing the risk to his or her future career on the playing field posed by an injury.

A potentially fatal block in an artery to the heart may no longer need the damaged vessel to be replaced with a vein taken from the leg. Instead, a tiny balloon can be inserted into the blood vessel, gently manoeuvred into position near the block and inflated to push it out of the way.

Keyhole surgery is still in its infancy. Future progress may depend at least in part on developments in one of the other high technology success stories of the 1980s – the laser – since this could replace the scalpel altogether in many operations.

5 Cutting rays

Where a fibreoptic tube can go, a laser beam will surely follow. When scientists first suggested over two decades ago that lasers might be used to destroy diseased tissue, their less adventurous medical colleagues thought they were mad. How could anything as powerful and dangerous as a laser beam ever be controlled sufficiently to be used in something as sensitive and precious as the human body?

Thousands of patients with conditions as wide ranging as diabetes, cervical cancer and heart disease have now benefited from the laser beam, proving the critics wrong.

A laser beam is produced when atoms are made to emit high energy rays of light. This energy is absorbed by human tissue and can generate enough heat to vaporize unwanted cells or seal bleeding vessels.

One of the earliest applications of lasers in medicine was to get rid of abnormal blood vessels in the eyes of people with diabetes. Left untreated, these vessels would leak blood on to the retina where images are focused and cause blindness. Surgery was difficult and not always successful. But with a laser, treatment is fast and effective.

Soon lasers were also being used to destroy early cancers of the cervix – the layer of tissue which separates the womb from the vagina in women. Once again the procedure was quick, effective and painless and significantly reduced the number of cases which progressed to more serious disease. Next, the laser beam was used to seal stomach ulcers and stop them bleeding.

A fine laser beam is used to drill a hole in one of the tiny bones deep inside the ear, in order to restore damaged hearing that resulted from an abnormal growth.

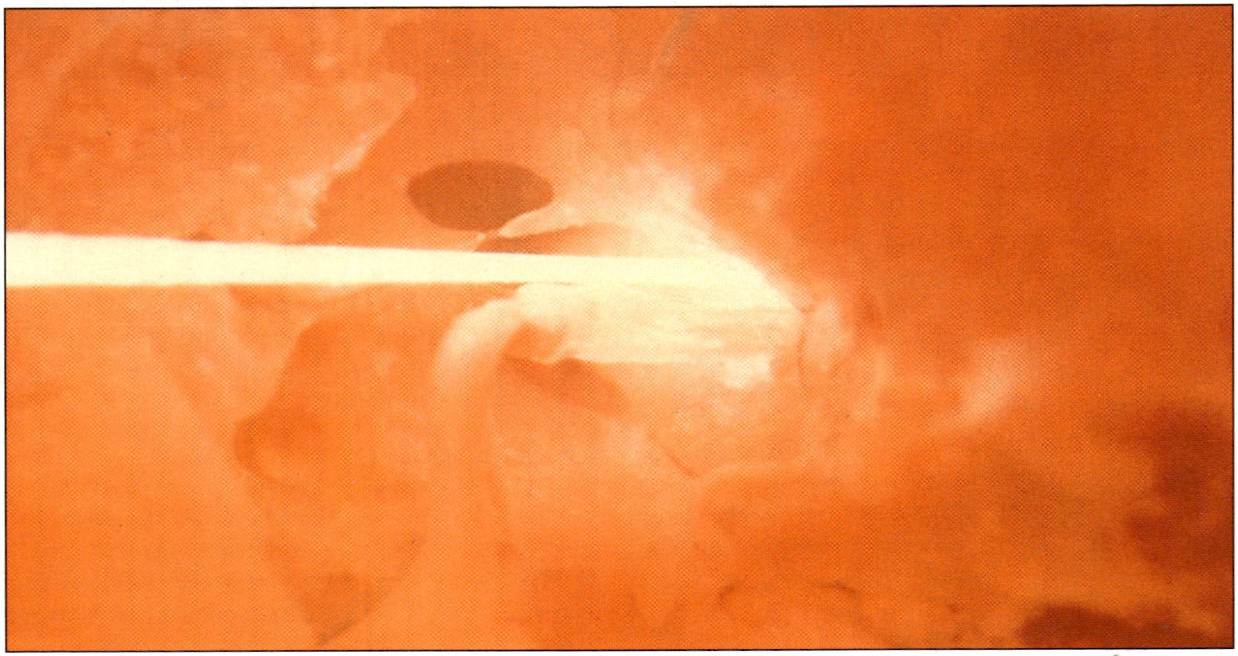

Right Laser beams are tested on different parts of a man's arm. Doctors are always trying to improve the effectiveness of their equipment.

Today, there are few parts of the body where lasers are not used. They can unblock arteries, nibble away at the lens of the eye and correct shortsightedness, even seek out and destroy some lung tumours when they are blocking vital airways.

Scientists are constantly refining the machinery needed to generate, carry and transmit the laser beam, so that it can be used in even more difficult situations, where scalpels cannot. Already, it has helped do away with many major operations which were difficult for surgeons to perform and very worrying for patients. And, before long, lasers could be used in the narrow, twisty, blocked and diseased blood vessels of the heart attack victim, demonstrating yet again their vital role in medical treatment.

6 Radiotherapy

The first cancer to be cured by radiotherapy was a nasal tumour in a Swedish patient. The year was 1899 and the form of radiation used was the X-ray. In the four years since Roentgen's discovery, numerous scientists had learned, to their cost, that X-rays could be used not only to take pictures of human tissue but also to destroy it. Their skin was covered in burns and many died years later as a result of exposure to radiation.

Radiotherapy, or radiation treatment, makes use of the destructive powers of rays. These are produced either electrically or from elements such as radium or cobalt-60, the atoms of which are unstable. Today, either X-rays or gamma rays may be used.

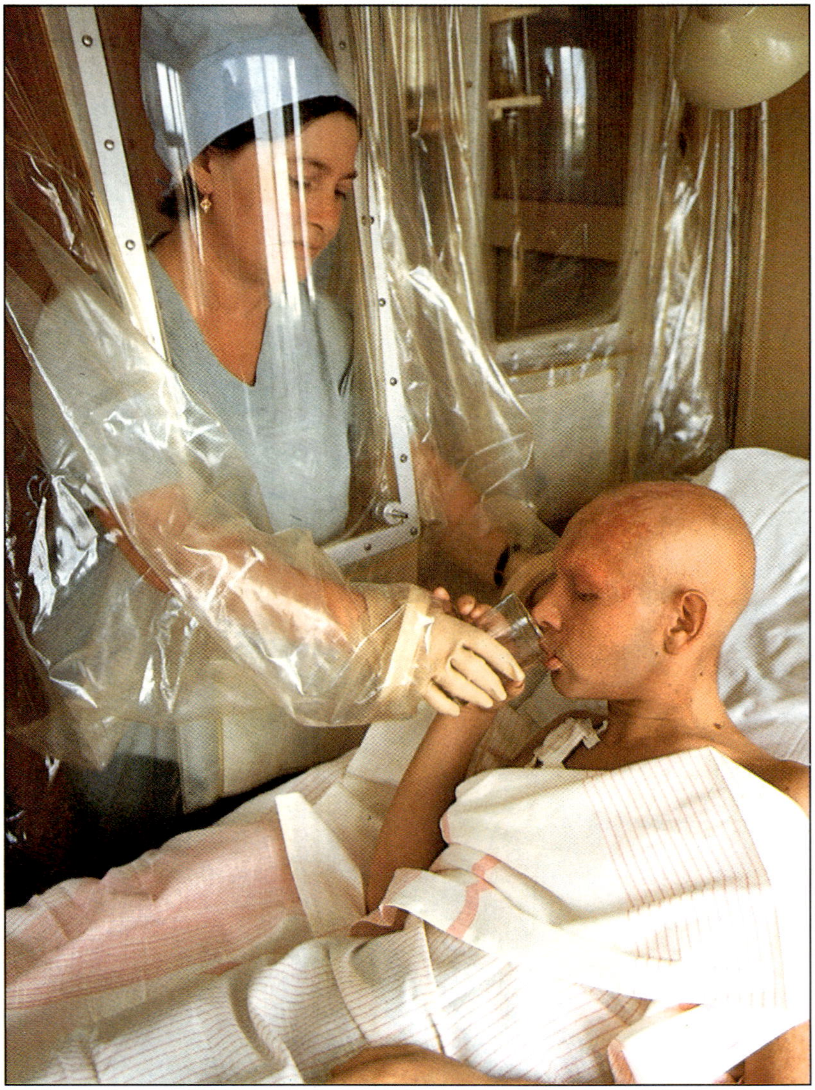

A victim of the Chernobyl nuclear disaster of 1986 is treated for radiation poisoning in hospital. Radio waves can kill as well as cure.

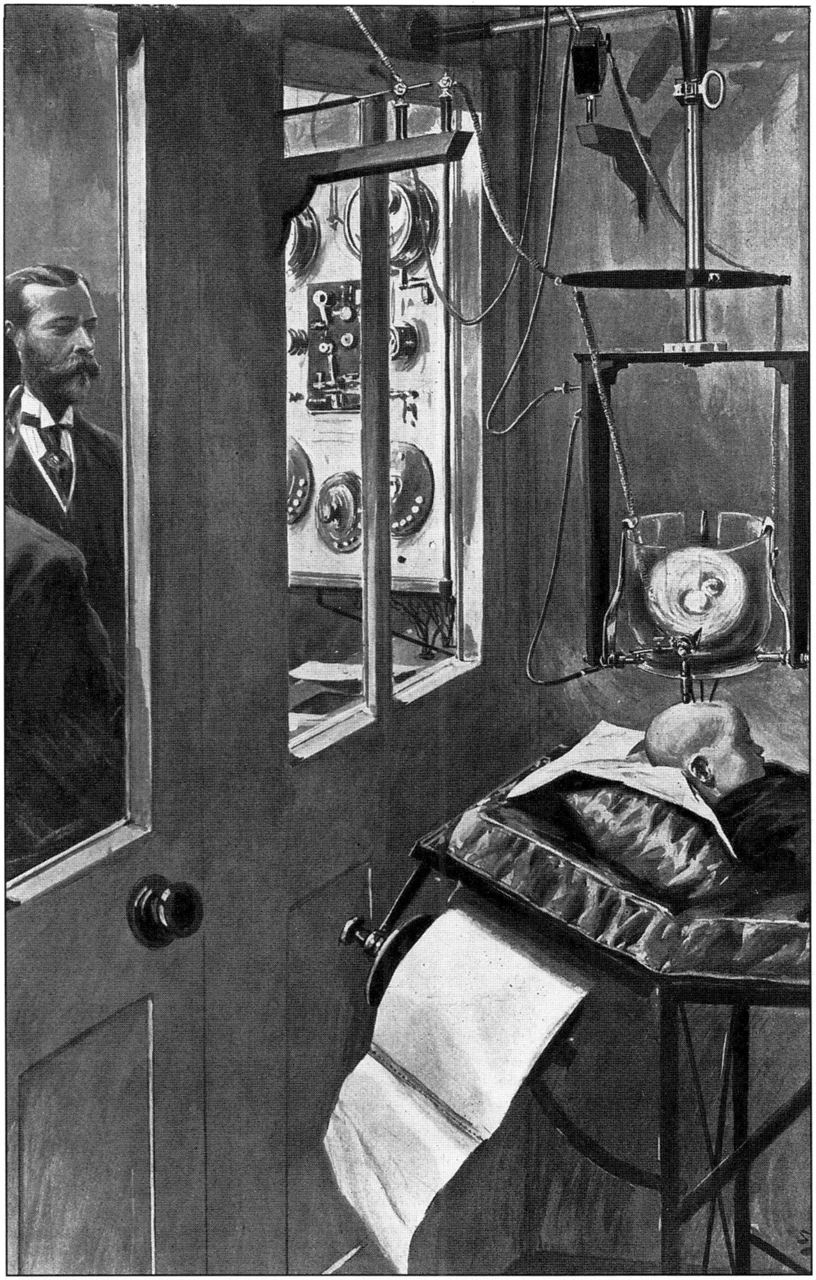

King George V of England watches an early attempt at radiotherapy at a London hospital in 1910.

X-rays and gamma rays destroy cancer cells by breaking up their structure, called DNA, and preventing them from multiplying.

Unfortunately, radiotherapy can also destroy normal cells. So the rays that are used have to be directed with pin-point accuracy at only the cancer cells. The dose is therefore calculated very precisely by computer and damage to surrounding healthy tissue is minimized by directing the beam from several directions. Think of the beam as a huge army of soldiers all meeting at the same place for a battle. By taking different routes they will get there more quickly and do less damage to the roads they are travelling on than if they all came the same way.

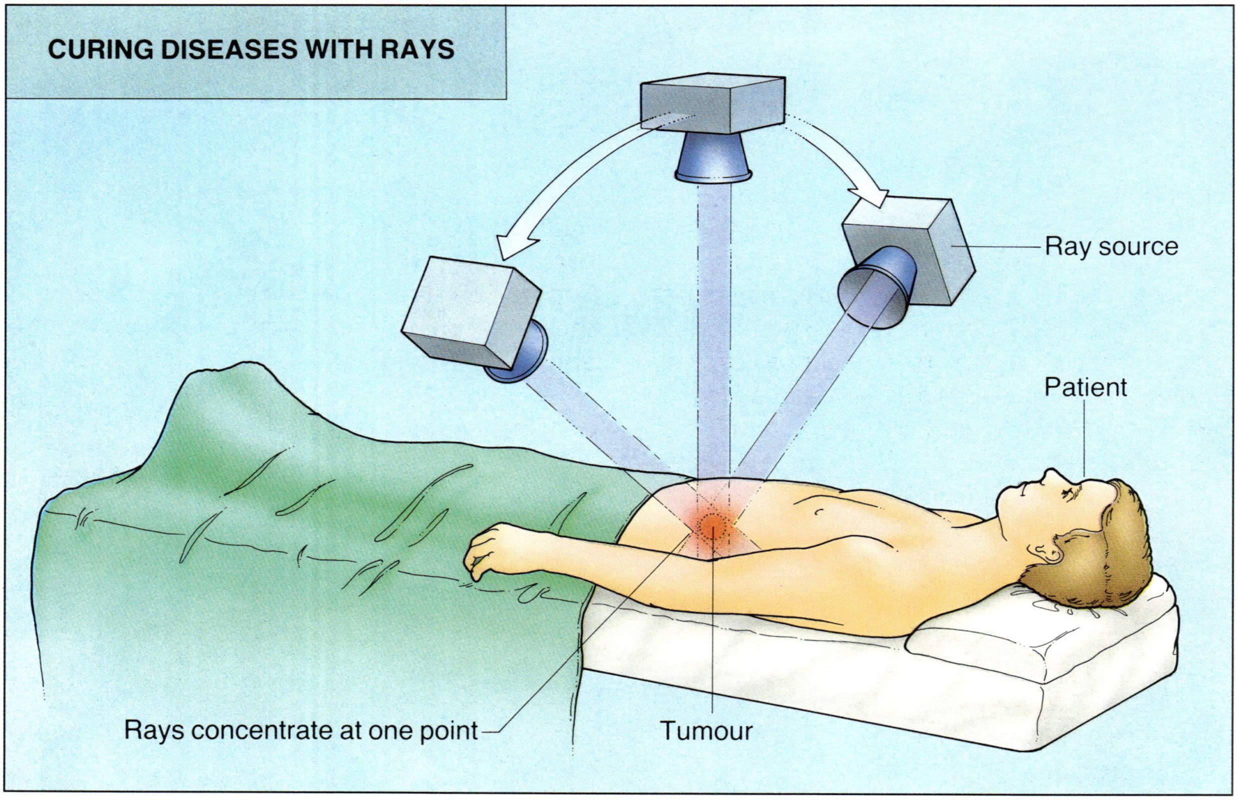

Above Radio waves are fired from several different directions so they do not damage healthy cells.
Below Lying under a radiotherapy unit can be a very frightening experience.

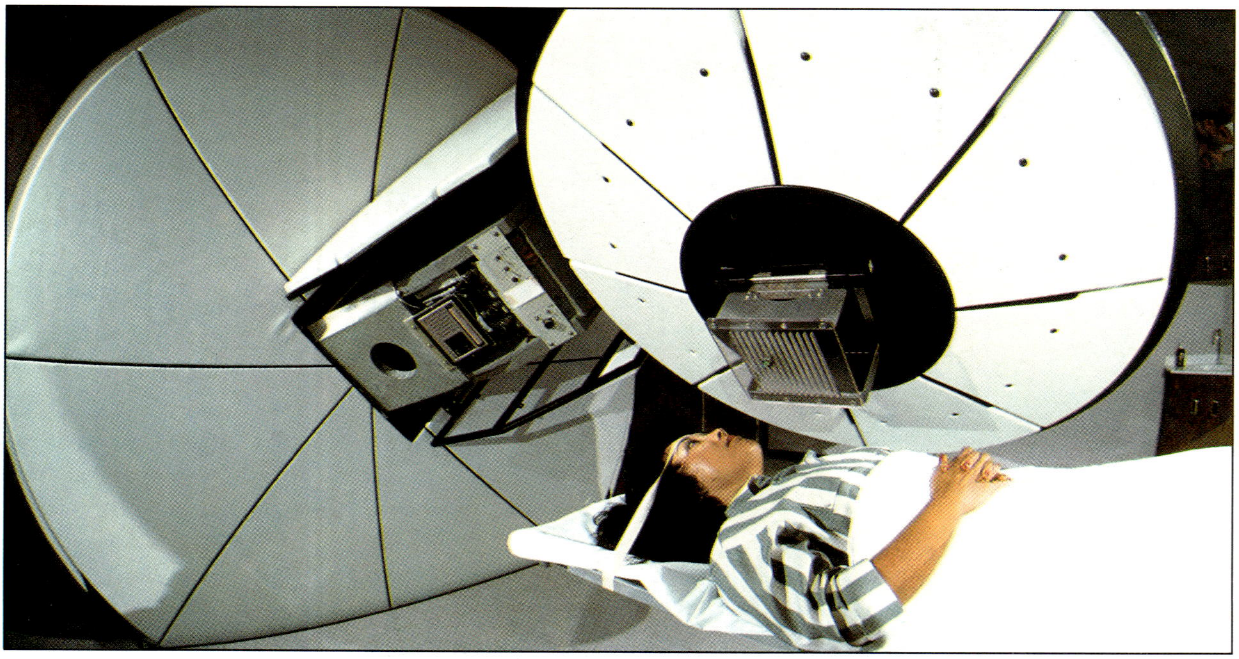

Radiotherapy is used most often against cancers which are difficult to remove surgically or are spread out through a large area. It is often used against head or neck tumours and cancer of the bladder.

It may also be used as palliative treatment; that is, to relieve symptoms rather than to cure the patient. Someone whose cancer has spread to their bones, for example, may suffer intense pain. Radiotherapy can be used to reduce the new tumours. It will not cure the patient but it will help to relieve the pain.

Radiotherapy is usually given as a course of treatment over several weeks and the rays delivered by a large external source of radiation. But, in some tumours, such as breast and womb cancers, radioactive wires can be implanted in the tissue and left to release their rays gradually over a few days.

Despite all the effort to ensure that radiotherapy destroys only cancerous tissue, some healthy cells are inevitably destroyed. Some patients experience unwanted effects of their treatment, such as tiredness, being sick and generally feeling unwell. Nevertheless, radiotherapy has played an important role in helping to increase the number of people who survive cancer.

Radioactive wires have been planted in the neck of this cancer patient as an alternative to a course of external radiotherapy over several weeks. The wires will be removed in a few days.

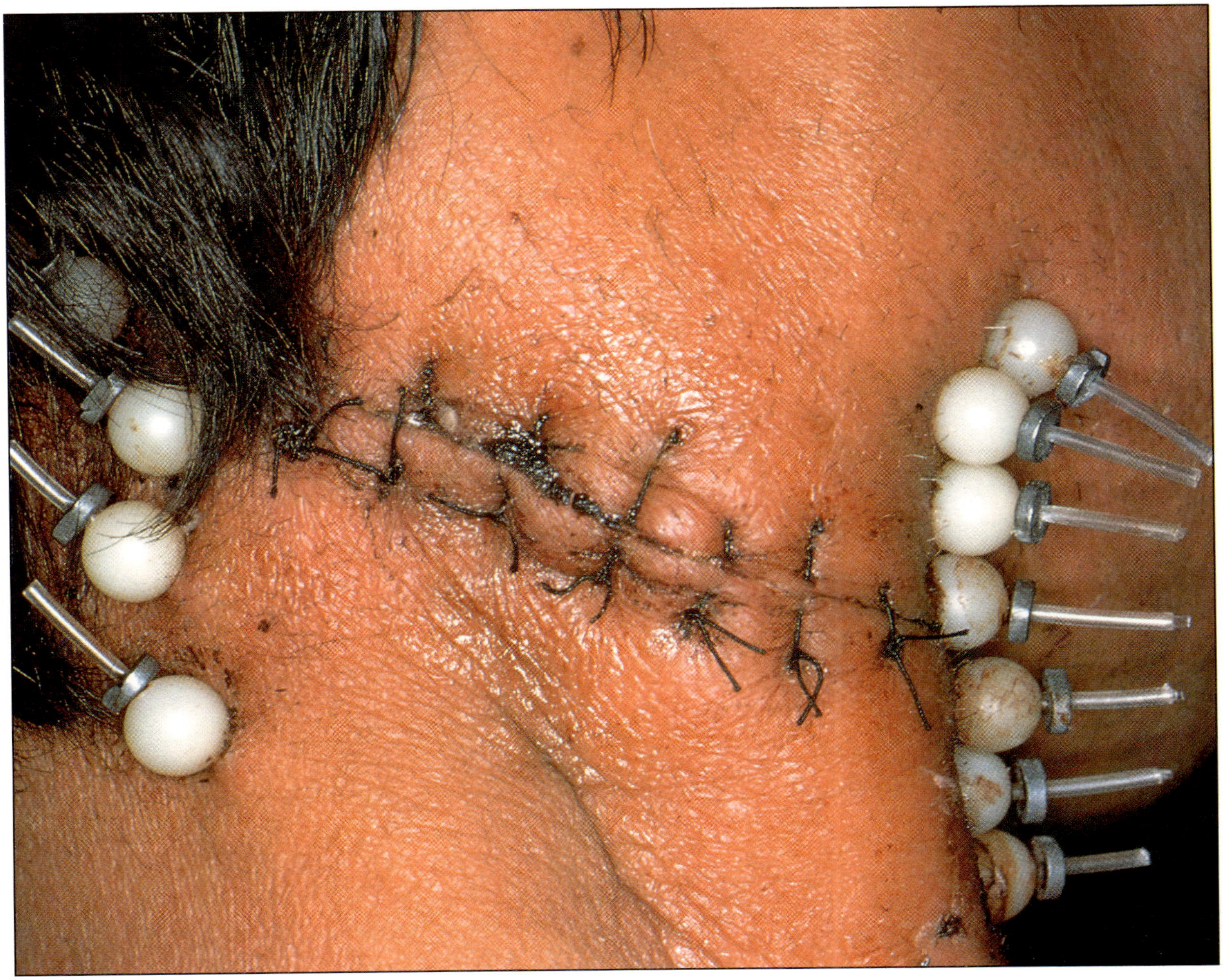

7 The healing power of light

Treating people with light can soothe their skin, lift their spirits, even save their life. Light therapy is widely used on its own, or with drugs, to heal both mind and body. In the last thirty years, scientists have discovered that several different kinds of light have health-giving effects.

Below An Italian picture from 1927. It shows ultraviolet light treatment for babies. Notice the sunglasses!

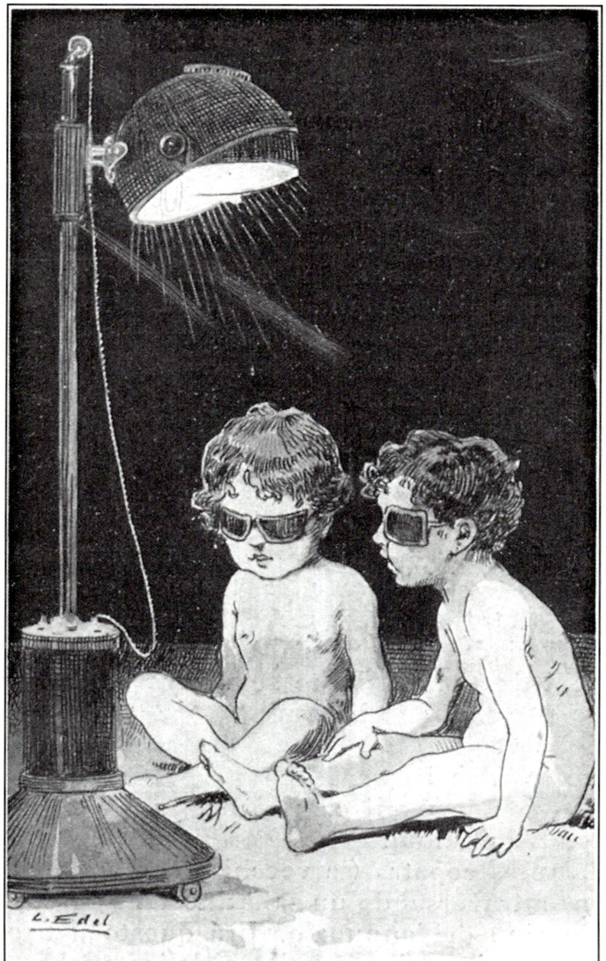

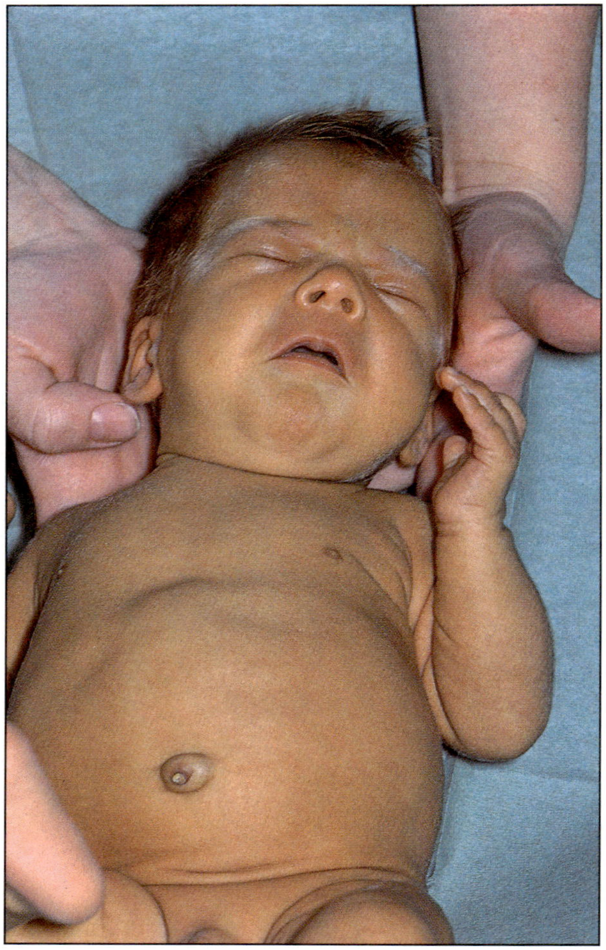

Above Jaundiced babies such as this one can be cured using sunlight.

Some babies are born with jaundice. This means that their liver is not working properly to break down worn out red blood cells. So yellow pigments from the cells build up in the skin. Exposing such babies to bright, natural light for a few days after birth stimulates their liver to start working properly and the yellow tinge to their skin gradually disappears.

Ultraviolet (UV) light is widely used to slow down the excessive production and shedding of skin cells which occurs in the condition called psoriasis. This is an unpleasant disease which leaves the sufferer's skin painfully inflamed and scaly. The treatment uses a drug called a psoralen, to make the skin of the patient sensitive to a type of UV light that restores the normal cycle of growth and decay.

The same combination of drug and UV light is also used to treat certain types of eczema and skin cancer. But great care has to be taken in controlling the amount of exposure to the light, since too much can cause cancer not cure it.

A growing number of people who suffer from seasonal affective disorder (SAD) – so-called 'winter depression' – are investing in specially designed fluorescent light strips which mimic, as closely as possible, natural daylight. People who suffer from SAD have linked their symptoms – depression, tiredness, poor concentration – to the lack of daylight during the winter months. They believe that, by boosting the amount of natural light in their home, they can trick the body into believing it is still summer.

These holidaymakers are relaxing and enjoying themselves in the sunshine. But the UV rays in sunlight that are used to treat some skin conditions can also cause cancer.

8 Kidney machines

People are born with two kidneys, even though they only really need one. Perhaps this is nature's way of giving us a back-up system. Sometimes, though, both of a person's kidneys stop working properly. When this happens, their blood has to be filtered – the job the kidneys normally do – in some other way.

The first attempts to build a machine which could do the work of the kidneys came in the USA in 1913. Experiments continued on both sides of the Atlantic throughout the 1920s, with little success. Finally, during the Second World War, a Dutch scientist, W J Kolff, managed to save the life of a patient who had acute (short-term) kidney failure. This achievement and his subsequent efforts to perfect the technique have resulted in Kolff being seen as the father of haemodialysis, which is the name given to the filtering of blood by machines.

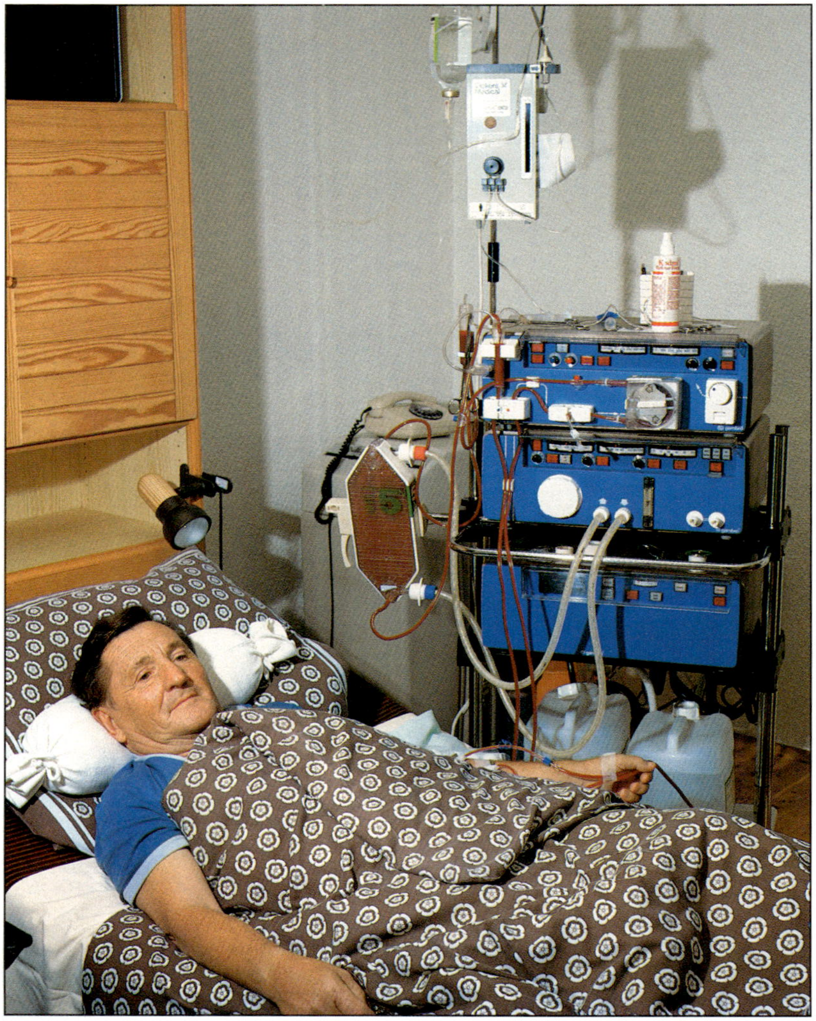

Home dialysis for patients with kidney disease helps reduce the need for hospital visits but can disrupt home life greatly.

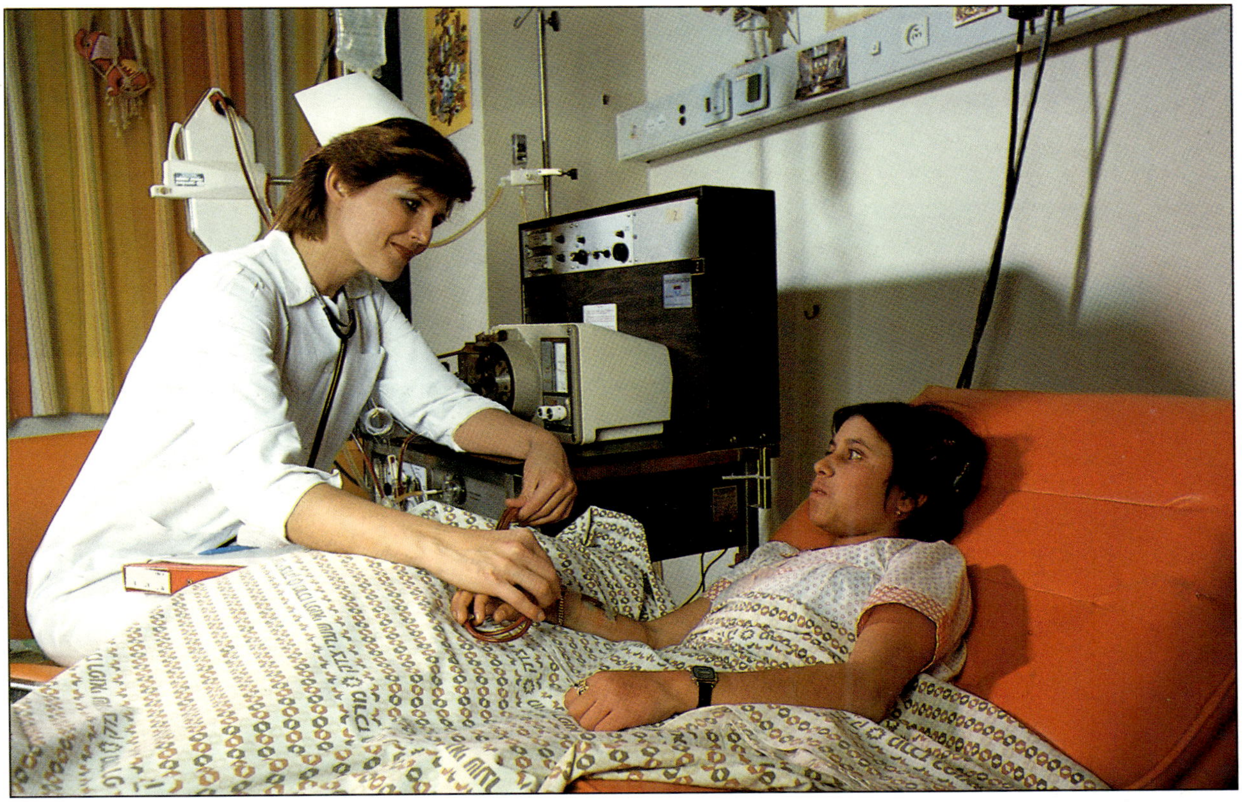

This woman is undergoing dialysis in hospital while she waits for a donor kidney to become available. Specially trained nurses care for such patients because the risk of infection is very high.

The kidneys are responsible for filtering waste products out of the blood and maintaining the balance of chemicals in the body fluids. The complexity of the process made it difficult to devise the perfect artificial kidney. Only since the mid-1960s have patients with chronic (long-term) kidney failure been offered regular dialysis on large bulky machines in order to clean their blood.

A tube is inserted into a blood vessel in the arm and blood passed through the dialysis machine. Waste products are removed and the blood is returned to the body through a second tube. The whole process takes several hours and has to be repeated every few days. Some patients have dialysis machines in their own home and they eventually get used to the routine.

Since the mid-1970s a small proportion of patients with chronic kidney failure have used an alternative method of cleaning their blood. Dialysis fluid is fed into the abdomen through a tube which carries it underneath the skin. Particles pass from tiny blood vessels called capillaries and into the dialysis fluid. Four times a day the fluid is drained out of the abdomen and replaced with a fresh supply. This takes only about an hour and can be done while the patient is involved in other activities. It is therefore much less restricting than conventional dialysis. But it does carry a greater risk of infection.

Both forms of dialysis tend to be considered as a temporary aid for patients with long-term kidney failure while they wait for a new kidney to become available for transplantation. There is really nothing to beat a human kidney!

9 The intensive care unit

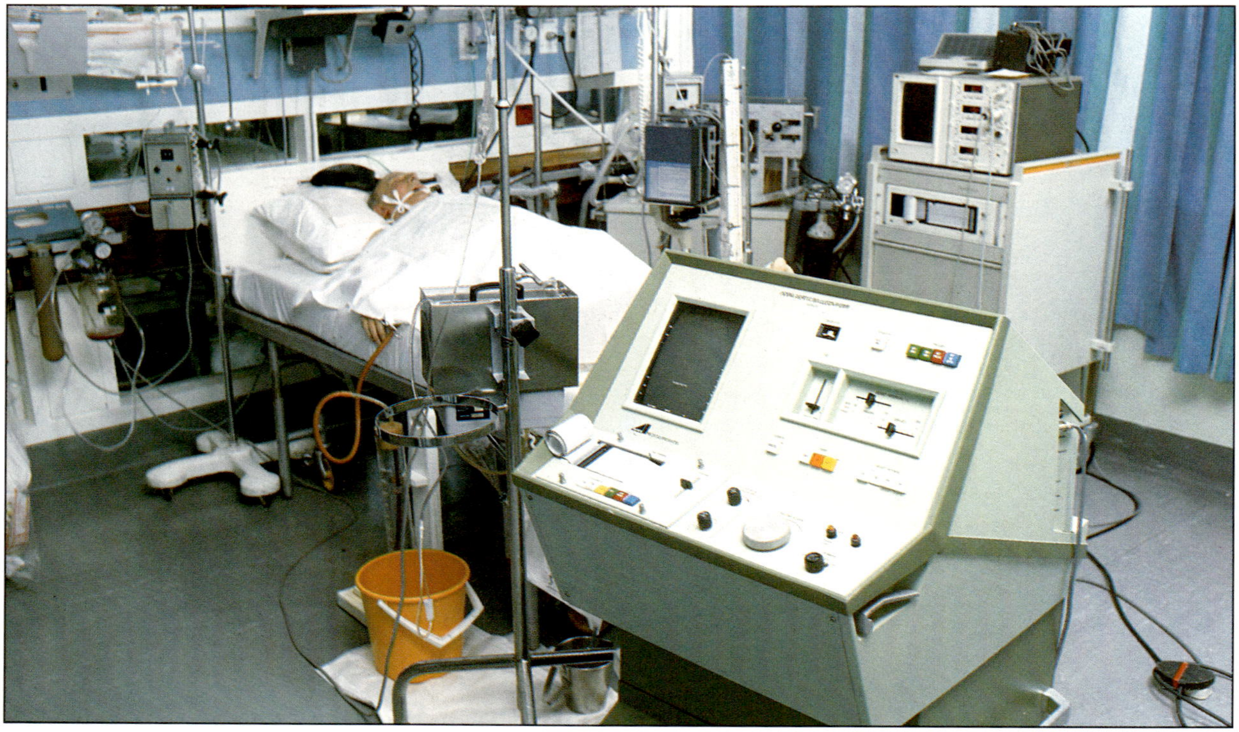

Very expensive equipment helps to keep this patient alive – machines monitor every breath he takes, while drugs are dripped into his bloodstream via a needle in his arm.

The intensive care unit (ICU) – also called the intensive therapy unit (ITU) – is a frightening place to the uninitiated. But, each year, thousands of patients in ICUs around the world owe their lives to the flashing, bleeping machines at their bedside. These include people who have had major surgery or been involved in a serious accident. Others have life threatening diseases of vital organs such as the heart, lungs or kidneys.

The treatment which can be given in ICUs is constantly being improved and updated so that people now survive injuries and diseases which only a few years ago would have meant certain death.

Care can be divided into two areas; monitoring and treatment. In order to decide what treatment is needed, doctors need to be able to measure minute by minute all the body's vital functions. This means the strength of the heart beat, how well the lungs are working, temperature in various parts of the body and urine production.

The machine most commonly used for treatment in the ICU is the lung ventilator. This usually involves inserting a tube directly into the upper airways of the lung, through a cut in the throat. The lungs can then be artificially inflated and deflated to mimic normal breathing.

Damage to one part of the body can have a knock-on effect in other areas. Many patients will suffer short-term kidney failure and need dialysis to clean their blood, despite the fact that their kidneys were not involved in the original injury or disease. Fortunately, once they recover from their illness, their kidneys are likely to start working again too. So they are unlikely to need long-term dialysis.

Since patients in ICUs may well be unconscious or very weak they will need all their food and liquids to be supplied directly into their bloodstream, via a tube. They are also likely to need a number of drugs, given by injection or through a drip into their arm.

ICUs are very labour intensive and expensive to run. Each patient needs his or her own nurse. Laboratory services must be available round the clock and mobile X-rays on call. Those who specialize in intensive care need extra training and there is a high burn-out rate because of the stress of working in a live or die atmosphere. But for those who can take the pace it can also be a very rewarding place to work.

Above An ambulance rushes a patient to the intensive care unit and the equipment that will save his or her life.

Below The parents of this premature baby will be grateful for the intensive care unit that is keeping her alive and kicking.

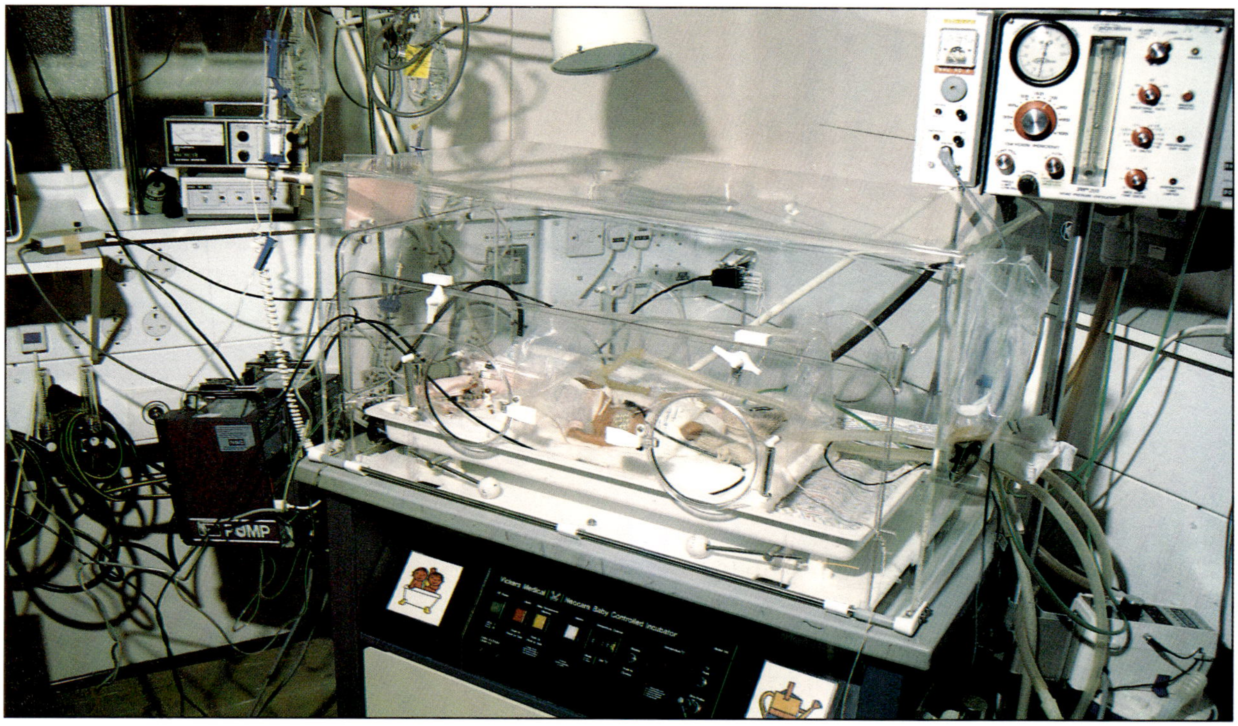

10 In the doctor's surgery

High technology medicine is not restricted to hospitals and specialist medical centres. More and more family doctors also use a wide range of automatic and computerized equipment. By doing many of the tests which used to need a hospital visit, doctors cut down on delays for patients waiting to find out what is wrong with them.

Many family doctors now have an electrocardiogram (ECG) machine which measures the electrical changes that occur during a heart beat. It is 95 per cent accurate in diagnosing a heart attack and also picks up abnormal heart rhythms, which may be a warning of future problems. A few family doctors also have a treadmill. They can use this to measure heart and lung function during exercise, in order to assess the overall performance of the heart and to diagnose heart failure – a chronic deterioration which, if left untreated, may be fatal.

Most doctors take blood samples and send them away to a laboratory for analysis. But some can now give us the results on the spot.

A growing number of family doctors are computerizing their practice, to make their record-keeping more efficient, so that they can provide a better service for their patients.

They use so-called 'desk-top' analysers which can test blood and urine samples for many abnormalities.

Although family doctors must be able to deal with a wide variety of minor ailments, and diagnose which require hospital treatment, some are now specializing in areas of medicine in which they are most interested. Pregnancy and childbirth is one of these and a doctor who offers this service may have a small ultrasound machine (see p.8) to monitor the fetus' progress in the womb.

All family doctors are being encouraged to computerize their practice. This means putting all their patients' records on computer discs instead of writing down their symptoms and treatment at each visit in their notes. This makes it much easier to work out who is due for a check-up.

High technology may have taken its time getting to the general physician's surgery, but now it is there, it is having an important impact.

Above Medicine in poor countries is often based as much on tradition as on science, because few people can afford Western technology.

Below Some doctors rely on traditional means of storing information.

11 Talking to a computer

How would you feel telling a computer about your illness and receiving your prescription on a print-out? Some hospitals and doctors' surgeries now use computer questionnaires – lists of questions and answers fed into a computer to get information from patients and help decide on treatment.

Patients, it seems, like the new type of consultation and often feel less inhibited in discussing personal problems with a computer. Questions appear on the computer screen and patients key in their answers. In general, they are given a series of options and asked to type 'yes' or 'no'. But some programmes allow them to give a more detailed description of their ailment.

Computer questionnaires use graphics too. A patient in pain, for example, may be given an outline of a human body on the screen and asked to shade the areas which hurt.

Some doctors use the questionnaires simply as a method of gathering information. It cuts down on the amount of time during the consultation which needs to be spent in taking the patient's medical history, and tends to gather more information than would normally be possible in a conventional interview. Other doctors actually use the programmes to make a tentative diagnosis.

Treatment is never based purely on what the computer says. But studies of patients with a number of different conditions, such as back pain and stomach ulcers, have shown a remarkable degree of agreement over the diagnosis between doctor and computer.

Because of this computers are being used increasingly to advise on treatment. Programmes are available which summarize the uses and doses of different drugs, their side-effects and the sorts of patients who should not take them.

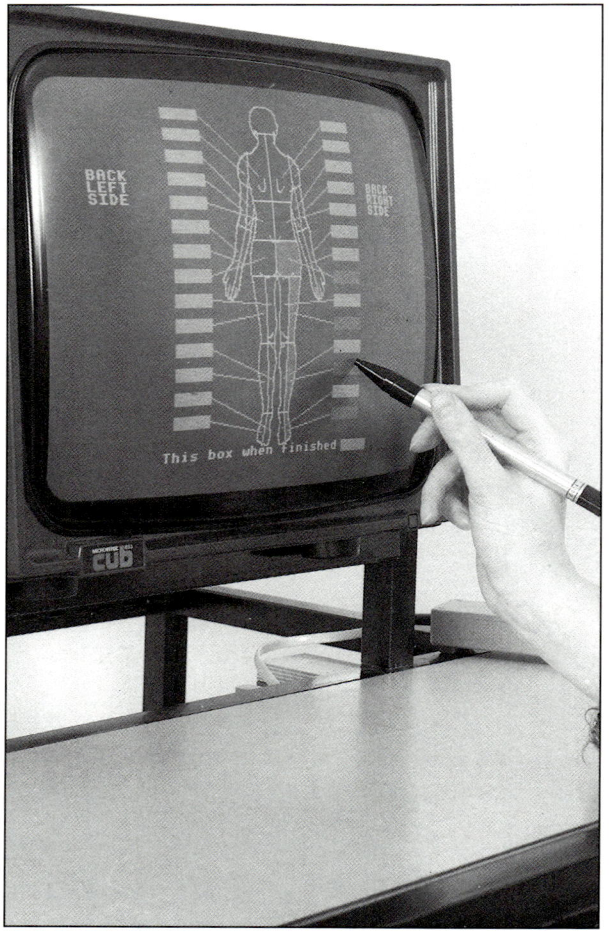

This patient is using a computer to explain how pain moves down her leg from her back; particularly useful for people who cannot speak.

In some areas, patients even leave their doctors' surgeries with a computer-printed prescription for their drugs. (Not a bad idea considering how many mistakes are made at the chemist's because of doctors' poor handwriting.) But, for the time being at least, it is the doctor who still decides what goes on the prescription.

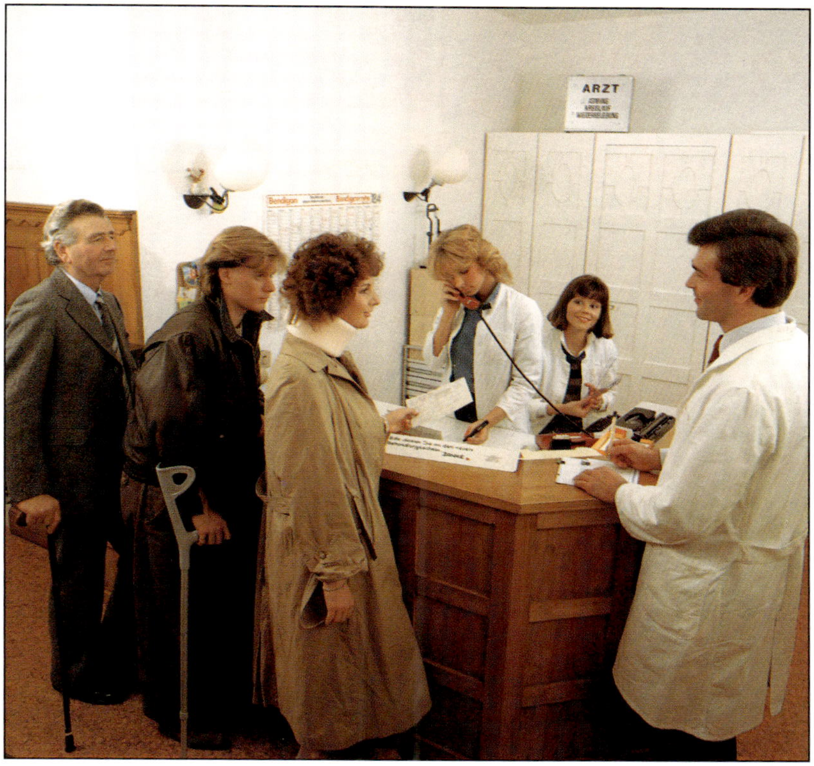

Right patients queue up for a more conventional interview with their doctor.

Left Medical students are shown how to interpret the data their patients put on computer.

12 Smart cards

By the time you are issued with your first credit card, you will probably already be carrying in your wallet a piece of plastic which looks like a credit card but actually contains a short history of your health.

The so-called smart card is already on trial in a number of countries. Each card has a computer chip capable of storing enough information for a doctor or pharmacist to judge what might be wrong with a patient and suggest treatment.

When a patient goes to the doctor or pharmacist the card is inserted into a computer, and the information it contains appears on the screen. When a decision about further treatment has been made the card can be updated.

This would be especially useful if, for example, a patient were taken ill while on holiday and it was impossible to contact his or her own doctor. At a glance, the new doctor could see whether the patient had a history

Today they queue up to use their cash cards to get money out of the dispenser. But in a few years they could be carrying similar cards containing details of their medical history.

On holiday abroad it would still be possible to get the right medical treatment if tourists carried smart cards detailing long-term illnesses and the drugs they needed.

of any particular illness and what treatment he or she was currently taking. It would help reduce the risk of a patient being given a drug which was unsuitable.

The information on the card is kept secret. Someone who picked up a card which has been lost or stolen would not have the equipment to read the information it contained. So there would be little risk of unauthorized people finding out about your medical conditions.

Researchers are still experimenting with how much information to put on the smart cards. They might prove to be a useful way of passing on information about a patient who is referred to hospital. Instead of notes having to be sent to the hospital, the patient could simply present the card at reception. The doctor would see immediately the nature of the medical problem and the treatment being received. It may even be feasible to put X-ray and other diagnostic pictures on to the cards.

At the press of a button on a card monitor your whole life will open up – from the moment of birth through to your latest cough or cold.

13 Technology in the home

Health care in the home now extends far beyond the medicine cabinet in the bathroom, with its plasters and headache pills. People with chronic conditions who, only twenty years ago, would have spent long periods of time in hospital can now live independently in the comfort of their own home. This is thanks to technological advances which enable them to monitor their progress and even adapt their treatment.

You have already read about patients with kidney failure who can get rid of waste products in their blood using dialysis machines at home (see p.22). Diabetics, cancer patients, people with heart problems and pregnant women are just a few of the other groups who have benefited from medical advances in the home.

People with diabetes have, for many years, monitored the amount of sugar in their blood by dipping paper strips containing diagnostic chemicals into samples of blood or urine. The strips change colour in response to the

Two different kinds of urine test for people with diabetes. **Above** This woman is able to use a home testing kit, while the school pupil **below** is shown how to perform the test in the clinic. She will soon be able to do it at home herself.

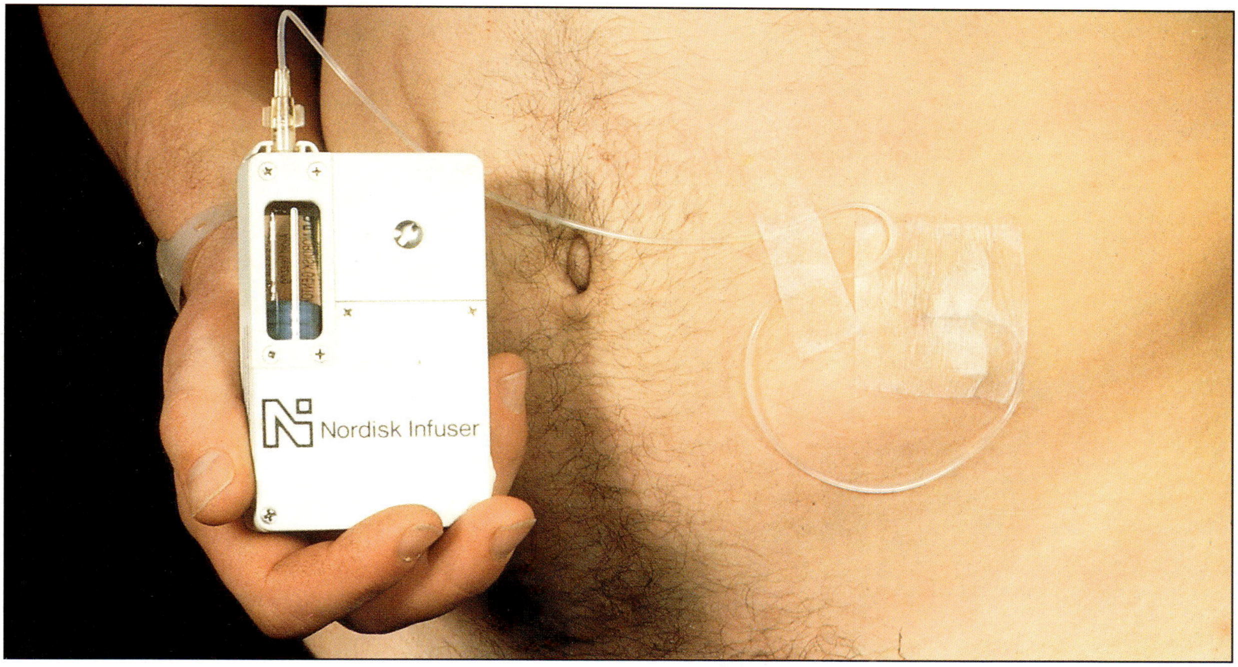

No need for frequent injections for this man. He has a pump that fits in a pouch round his waist and drips insulin into his bloodstream to control the amount of sugar in his blood.

amount of sugar in the sample. Too much sugar and the diabetic knows that he or she needs to increase the dose of insulin – the hormone that normally controls the amount of sugar released.

Recently, however, a number of machines have been developed which measure the amount of sugar in the sample automatically. The patient may get a visual display of the result, a print-out, or even a spoken result – especially useful for those with poor vision. The device comes in all shapes and sizes. Some, shaped like pens or credit cards, can even be carried around in the pocket.

At any time, there are a large number of people with cancer living at home. Many are undergoing courses of anti-cancer drugs or need regular, effective treatment to control their pain. Some now rely on pumps – about the size and shape of a personal stereo – which drip the drugs they need directly into their bloodstream while they carry on their daily activities.

A tiny tube is implanted into a blood vessel in the patient's chest so that drugs can be taken in continuously. The devices have to be very accurate but they can be adapted when delivering pain-killing drugs so that the patient can increase or decrease the amount of drug according to how well he or she feels.

Some people with high blood pressure carry a device like a personal stereo around with them. And these actually contain a cassette! The machine records blood pressure constantly and makes a permanent record of the results for later analysis by the doctor.

Blood pressure is subject to large variations depending on whether someone is asleep, sitting down or exercising. For someone with high blood pressure which is difficult to control, it may be important to know precisely what levels it is likely to reach during the day so that the most effective treatment can be given. Simply measuring the blood pressure in the doctor's surgery when the patient is relatively relaxed is not enough.

A telephone call allows this woman to transmit the fetus's heartbeat to the hospital

A growing number of people are buying their own blood pressure measuring machines for use in the home – either out of curiosity or because they are having treatment for heart or circulatory problems. Their accuracy does vary considerably and there is really no substitute for having your blood pressure measured by an expert.

You do not have to be ill to take advantage of medical technology in the home. Pregnant women can telephone their fetus's heart beat to the hospital and thus avoid the need for lots of hospital check-ups. The technique tends to be used mainly by women whose fetuses are thought to be at risk. This could be because they have had one or more previous miscarriages or because the fetus is not growing properly.

Such women have an ultrasound system at home which records the fetus's heartbeat in the womb. The heartbeat is then coded so that it can be transmitted down a telephone line. At the hospital, the recording is decoded and printed out as a graph of the electrical changes in the heart. Specialists can examine the graphs and see immediately if there are any problems which mean that the woman needs to be brought into hospital for treatment.

As we reach the end of the twentieth century a number of factors have combined to make it increasingly important that, wherever possible, people are treated at home. The costs of medical care in hospital are soaring and, as the proportion of people who reach old age increases, the demands on health services worldwide will become ever more difficult to fulfil. By treating more patients in their home, health care providers hope that they can not only help improve the quality of life for patients but also reduce the cost of looking after an ageing population.

Below Increasing medical technology will allow old people to stay well at home. This will reduce the cost of health care.

14 Bionic men and women

WORLD NEWS

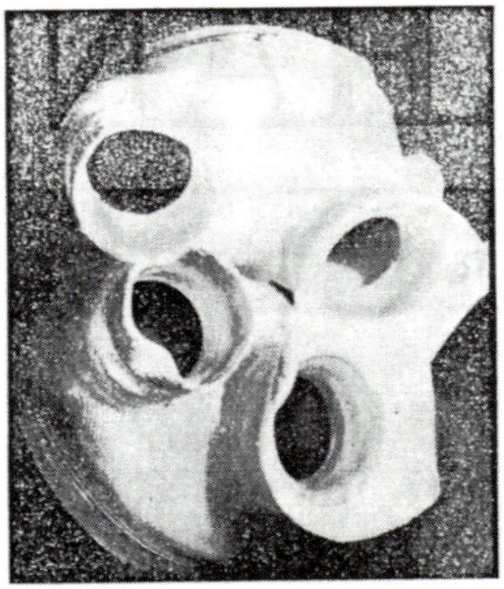

The plastic heart that beats in Dr Clark

First plastic heart saves a dying man

AMERICA

Dr Clark . . . "doing well"

By PHILIP FINN

A DYING man was given the world's first artificial heart yesterday.

And just a few hours after the plastic organ was implanted in the 61-year-old former dentist, the hospital said :—

"Now he has the blood pressure of an 18-year-old man and is doing very well."

The six-hour operation on father - of - three Dr Barney Clark at the University of Utah's medical centre, was dramatically brought forward when his diseased heart slowed to "barely a quiver."

It will be three days before the 20-strong team of surgeons, led by Dr William Devries, can be sure the device has not been rejected.

The £12,500 heart, designed to support life indefinitely, is being driven by compressed-air hoses.

They replace the heart muscles that beat 40 million times a year.

That means Dr Clark, from Washington, must be connected by plastic tubes to a portable compressor for the rest of his life.

The heart, called "Jarvik-Seven," was named after inventor Dr Robert Jarvik, of the university, who had only tested it in animals.

A university spokesman said : "Whether it goes well, or ill, we will learn from it. For Dr Clark it was his last chance."

Last night in Cape Town, South Africa, heart-swop pioneer, Professor Christian Barnard, said : "The Utah device does not seem to be the solution — real transplants are the answer."

The man 'saved' in this operation died months later. Other patients who have had similar operations are sueing the makers of their valves, because so many have failed.

In the 1970s a popular television series called *The Six Million Dollar Man* told of an astronaut whose spaceship crashed. His injuries were so great that he had to be 'rebuilt' using electronic parts. At the time such a cure seemed impossible, but it has since begun to be closer and closer to reality.

Hearts, kidneys, livers, lungs, and joints can all now be replaced with varying degrees of success. But these operations would not be possible without behind-the-scenes advances in technology. These are often overlooked when the spotlight is focused on the undoubted skills of the surgeons performing the transplants.

Before any organ is transplanted it has to be 'tissue typed' to make sure that it matches as closely as possible the patient's tissues, otherwise it will be rejected. The scientists look for the proteins on the surface of the donor's cells. These are capable of causing the organ to be rejected if they are not carefully matched with those of the patient. They are called human leucocyte antigens.

Once a match has been made it is vital that the donor organ is kept in the best possible condition before it is transplanted. Ideally, donor and recipient should be in next door operating theatres so that the organ can be transferred directly. But since this is rarely possible the organ must be carefully cooled and stored in ice. A kidney will last for up to forty-eight hours if preserved correctly, a liver for ten and a heart for just four hours.

Access to technology is of vital importance during a transplant. During heart and lung transplants all the patient's blood has to be pumped around his or her body artificially.

It may seem like an artificial vampire, sucking out patients' blood, but this machine is crucial during open heart surgery to pump blood around the body.

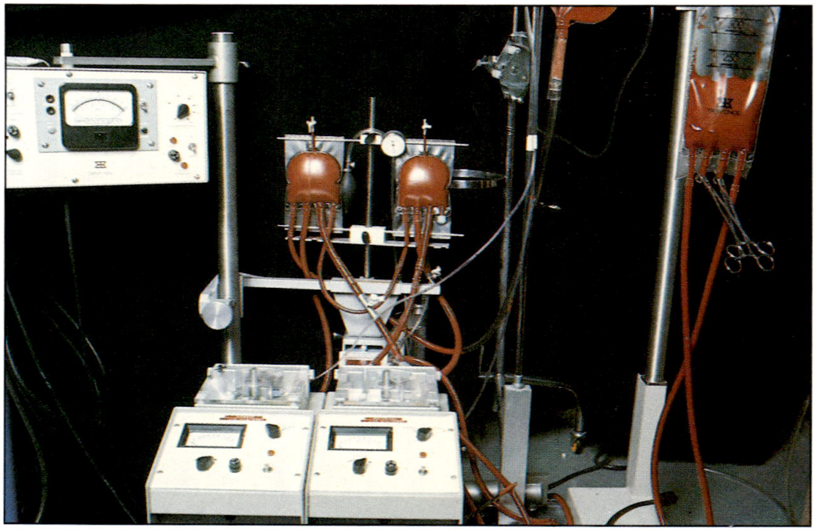

Without a heart/lung bypass machine it would be impossible to perform the delicate surgery that is needed.

Some surgeons are experimenting with artificial hearts – usually as a stop-gap while they wait for a suitable human organ for transplantation. A small pump is implanted in the chest and connected to a machine at the patient's bedside which stimulates it to push the patient's blood around the body. Such systems are very dangerous for the patient, because blood clots can form on the surface

Patients who have had joint replacements need extensive rehabilitation to get their limbs working.

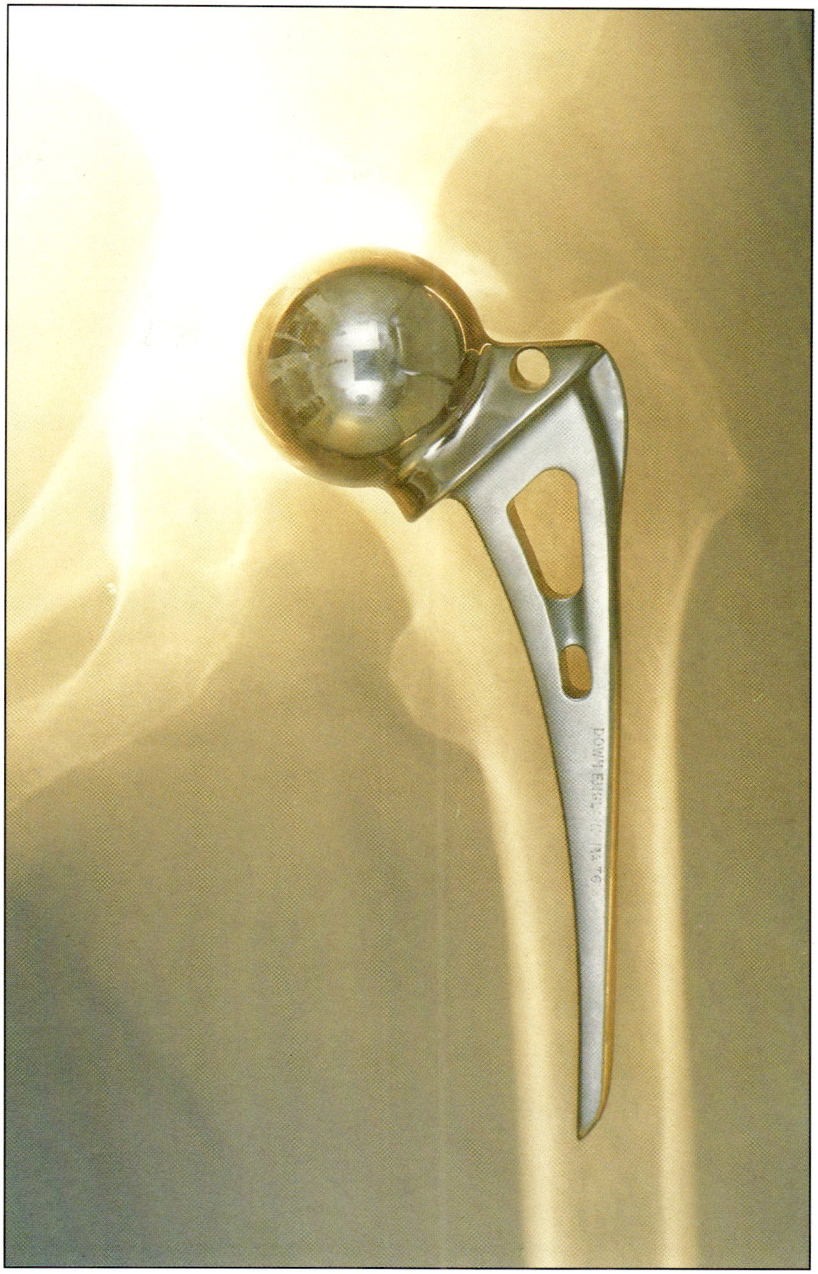

This picture gives an idea of the position of an artificial hip joint after it has been inserted. The patient would now be able to walk normally.

of the artificial devices, causing death. This is why they are unlikely, in the foreseeable future, to take the place of human hearts.

Artificial materials have been used much more successfully in replacing worn out joints. Each year, thousands of elderly people have replacements of hip, knee, hand and foot joints and, increasingly, shoulder and elbow joints too. The materials used for the new joint and for fixing it in place are constantly being re-evaluated to improve performance and durability and reduce the risk of infection.

The prediction, 'We can rebuild him' at the start of *The Six Million Dollar Man* is fast becoming a reality!

15 Babies from the test-tube

Thousands of test-tube babies have been born since that remarkable day in 1978 when Louise Brown was born. She was the first child to come into the world who had been conceived outside her mother's womb. Since then great progress has been made in perfecting and extending the technique so that more infertile couples can benefit from in vitro fertilization (IVF) as it is called.

The basics are still the same now as then. The woman is given hormones to make her produce one or more eggs in her ovaries. These are removed through a small incision in her abdomen and mixed, in the laboratory, with sperm from her partner. If all goes well the sperm will fertilize the eggs and these will start to divide to form tiny embryos. These clusters of cells will be examined and some of the healthiest ones replaced in the woman's womb.

Daily Mail

THURSDAY, JULY 27, 1978 8p

WORLD EXCLUSIVE

And here she is...

THE LOVELY LOUISE

An important day for infertile couples: the birth of the first test-tube baby.

Test-tube baby pioneer Robert Edwards proudly holds up the 2,500th test-tube baby. Advances in IVF have been shared internationally, with countries such as Australia taking a lead.

Doctors now know that the more embryos they put back the greater the chances of a successful pregnancy. Alternatively, they can keep back some of the embryos and freeze them so that the couple can have another attempt at having a test-tube baby at a later date.

One variation of IVF is GIFT – gamete intra-fallopian transfer. Eggs are removed from the woman's ovaries, mixed with sperm and immediately replaced in one of the woman's fallopian tubes, which join the ovaries to the womb. It is a simpler method which does not need so much laboratory back-up. But if it does not work it is harder to work out why.

Despite all the excitement about test-tube babies it has to be remembered that only a small proportion of women who have the treatment actually give birth. Many couples try for years without success, which is very sad for them. This is why research into better ways of performing IVF is continuing. Scientists also need answers to the many ethical questions which have arisen. What should happen to the extra embryos which are not replaced in the mother's womb? Should they be destroyed, used for research or simply stored? Who gets custody of frozen embryos if a couple get divorced? Advances in technology such as IVF – while they must be welcomed – also raise dilemmas which only society can resolve.

16 Genetic engineering

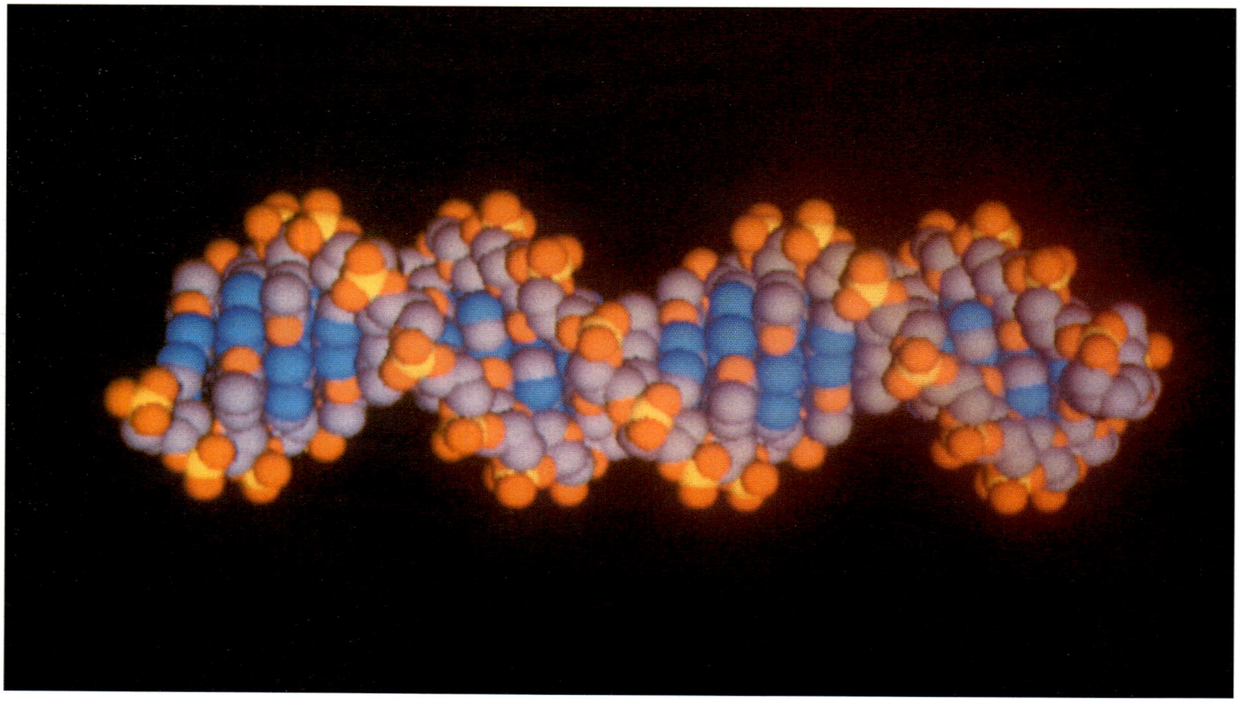

The code for an individual's entire physical make-up – passed down from his or her parents – is contained in double helical structures that look like this, called DNA.

In 1953 Dr James Watson and Dr Francis Crick predicted that their discovery of the structure of DNA would have important implications for the future. But they cannot have guessed how far reaching those implications would be. Nor that they would live to see their discovery being used to find not only the cause of many life threatening diseases but also ways of treating them.

DNA (deoxyribonucleic acid) is a string of molecules contained in the body's cells, which holds the genetic code for all of an individual's physical and mental characteristics. By discovering its structure, Watson and Crick had found the key which would enable scientists to unlock the mystery of what makes us tick – and how to change us.

It was more than a quarter of a century after Watson and Crick's discovery that scientists found how to manipulate DNA in order to change someone's genetic make-up. Even today it is only microscopic organisms that have their genes routinely changed and moved about.

The genes of bacteria, for example, have been engineered to make them produce human proteins such as insulin and growth hormone, which they would not normally do. In effect, microscopic organisms such as bacteria can be turned into production lines for many vital human proteins that cannot be made easily in any other way.

Genetic engineering, as this process is known, has also been used to help pin-point the genes that cause serious inherited disorders such as haemophilia, muscular dystrophy or cystic fibrosis.

This has meant that babies likely to suffer one of these can be identified in the womb and their parents offered the opportunity of ending the pregnancy. Eventually, scientists would like to be able to correct these abnormal genes so that such problems can be wiped out altogether.

But, as with IVF, scientists are aware of the need for ethical guidelines to control the genetic experiments which can be done and to tell them how far they should go in trying to create the perfect human being.

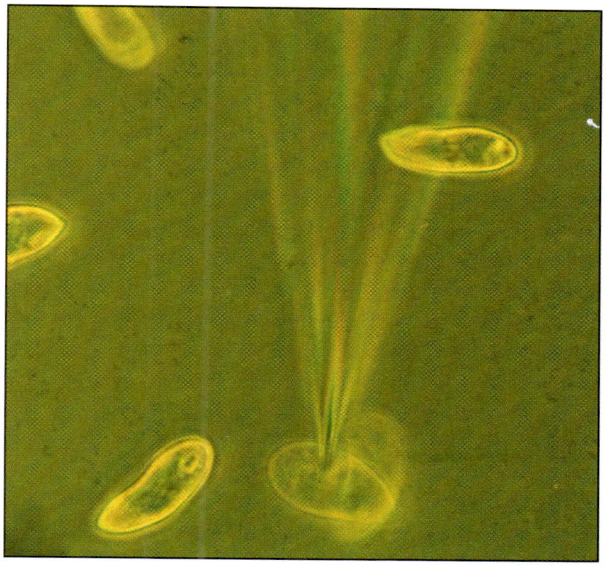

Above DNA is transferred into a single cell organism so that its genes can be changed to make proteins useful to humans.

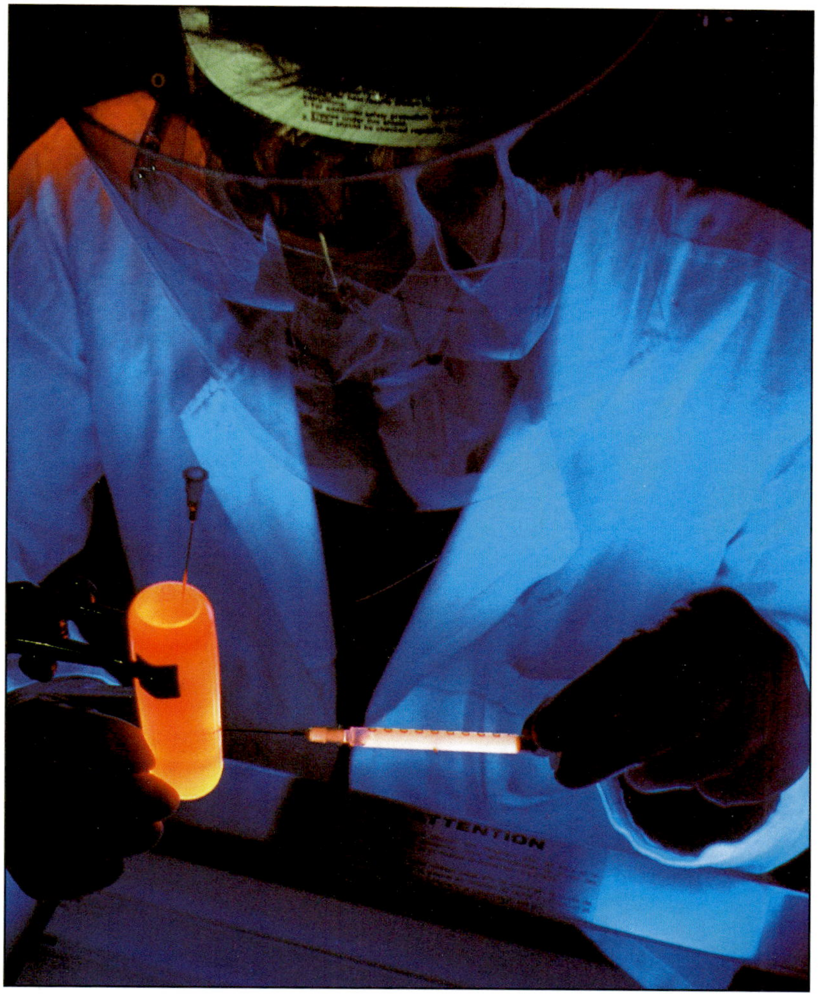

Left Here, DNA is being extracted from human white blood cells so that it can be examined for abnormalities.

17 Brave new world

Where does medical technology go from here? We have the tools to begin life in the laboratory, to adapt it to our needs and to prolong it well beyond the 'three score and ten years' (or seventy years) we were allotted in the Bible.

But are we using this technology in the right way? The majority of people in the world are denied access to even basic health care, because they live in poor countries. They cannot afford the expensive equipment that the rich countries have developed.

Each year millions of children die from malnutrition and infections, which can easily be prevented. They would benefit from vaccines and drugs developed through genetic engineering and other high-technology methods. For most companies,

A modern hospital such as this one in Canada costs millions of pounds to build and run. It offers those in rich countries the very latest in diagnosis and treatment of disease.

Left Contrast the difference between the hospital far left and this hospital for victims of the Ethiopian civil war.

Below Guns or medicines? Unicef is an international organization that helps poor children get food, education and health care. Do you think money spent on bombs should be given to Unicef instead?

however, preventing or treating tropical infections such as malaria or sleeping sickness comes low on the list of priorities. It is much easier to go on producing more and better drugs to fight Western ills – heart disease, cancer and the degenerative diseases of old age – which people can afford to pay for.

This is bringing us a population crisis no less serious than that facing many poor countries. A huge increase in numbers of elderly people will have to be looked after, while the number of young people in the poor countries goes up and up.

There is a grave danger that as medical technology tries to satisfy the ever-increasing expectations of the world's wealthy, the gap between rich and poor will grow ever bigger.

We must begin to ask whether our knowledge is doing as much good as possible, or whether it is being abused. Is it time we took seriously the World Health Organization pledge of 'Health for All by the Year 2000' and used our technology to help achieve it?

Glossary

Antibiotics. Drugs, such as penicillin, which combat infections caused by bacteria.
Artery. A blood vessel which carries blood with oxygen in it around the body.
Arthritis. An inflammation of the joints that leads to pain and stiffness.
Asthma. A narrowing of the airways to the lungs that leads to breathing difficulties.
Bacteria. A type of microscopic organism.
Bladder. The organ in the abdomen in which urine is stored.
Cartilage. The tough tissue found in the joints, which acts as a shock absorber during movement.
Chromosomes. The thread shaped structures, grouped in pairs around all cells, which carry the genetic information that controls all of an individual's physical and mental characteristics at birth.
Cystic fibrosis. A common, severe inherited disorder in which mucus is found throughout the body, especially the lungs and digestive system, leading to blockage and an increased risk of infection.
Diabetes. A disease caused by failure of the pancreas to produce the hormone insulin, which is involved in breaking down sugar in the bloodstream.
Diagnosis. The identification of a disease or medical condition.
Dialysis. The use of a machine to do the work of the kidneys.
Discs. The flexible pads of tissue which separate the bones of the spine.
DNA (deoxyribonucleic acid). The molecules which carry the genetic code of a person's physical and mental make-up.
Eczema. An inflammation of the skin that causes soreness and redness.
Element. A basic chemical, such as carbon or hydrogen, which cannot be broken down into any other substance.
Embryo. The early stage of human development in the womb, between two and eight weeks after conception.
Fetus. The second stage of human development in the womb, lasting from eight weeks after conception until birth.
Fibreoptics. The fine plastic or glass tubes used to carry images from inside the body up to an eyepiece.
General anaesthetic. The drug used in major operations to make sure the patient cannot feel pain.
Haemophilia. A serious, inherited disorder that stops blood from clotting. Sufferers do not stop bleeding.
***In vitro* fertilization.** The fertilization of the female egg outside the body.
Local anaesthetic. A drug used in some operations to stop the patient feeling pain in a particular place.
Miscarriage. The accidental and premature ending of a pregnancy.
Multiple sclerosis. The gradual degeneration of the nerves, which leads to paralysis and disability.
Muscular dystrophy. An inherited disease that causes the muscles to waste away.
Ovary. Female organ in the lower abdomen where eggs are made.
Pharmacist. A person who is trained to understand how medicines are made and how they affect the body.
Scalpel. A surgeon's operating knife.
Treadmill. A moving walkway, used to measure a person's fitness and heart and lung function.
Tumour. An abnormal growth of cells, which can either be limited to one place or able to spread to other parts of the body.
Vagina. The passage in a woman's body up to the cervix and the womb.

Further reading

For children
Cartwright, FF, *A Social History of Medicine* (Longman, 1977)
Hardie, Averie and Wells, *Making Sense of Science: Human Biology* (Longman 1981, revised 1989)
Lambert, M, *Medicine in the Future* (Wayland, 1986)
Medawar, P, *Advice to a Young Scientist* (Pan, 1981)

For adults
Hayward, G, *Applied Genetics* (Macmillan, 1990)
Solomon, EP, and Phillips, G, *Understanding Human Anatomy and Physiology* (WB Saunders, 1987)
Taylor, J, *Microorganisms and Biotechnology* (Macmillan, 1990)

Acknowledgements

All artwork is supplied by Nick Hawken.

The publishers would like to thank the following for allowing their photographs to be reproduced in this book: Counsellor 32 (both); Mary Evans 4, 6, 17, 20 (left); Eye Ubiquitous 21, 27 (top), 30, 31, 34 (right); John Frost 35, 38; *General Practitioner* 26; Hutchison 8 (bottom), 42; Photri 29 (bottom); Dr Francis Pynsent 28; St Mary's Hospital 20 (right); Science Photo Library 9, 11, 14, 19, 33, 40, 51 (left); Tony Stone 5 (top), 15; Topham 34 (left), 39, 43 (top); Wayland 5 (bottom), 12 (top), 27 (bottom), 43 (bottom); Zefa *cover*, 8 (top), 12 (bottom), 13, 15, 19 (bottom), 22, 23, 24, 25 (both), 29 (top), 36 (both), 37, 41 (right).

Index

Entries that appear in **bold** refer to both text and pictures.